A

DALLAS WILLARD

DICTIONARY

ELANE O'ROURKE

FOR THE APPRENTICES

ACKNOWLEDGEMENTS

Dallas Willard's work in Christian philosophy and spiritual formation has inspired generations of disciples. The primary purpose of this book is to assist his readers in gaining deeper understanding of his writings and ideas. Hence the content of this book would have been neither relevant nor possible without him. I am profoundly grateful to him for his tireless work, his gentle humanity, and his love of God.

Special thanks to Dr. Gary W. Moon, Executive Director of the Dallas Willard Center and director of the Renovaré Institute of Spiritual Formation, for his welcome and encouragement. Gary and the members of the Denver Cohort are the reason this book got written at all. Most especially I give thanks to and for Lacy Borgo, Kevin Tupper, and Ross Tatum, who made me feel that it might matter.

Thanks to Bill Gaultiere for his critique and advice, and to Jane Willard for her kind words.

To Becky and Bill Heatley, who provided much of the resource material and insight. They are faithful curators of Dallas' papers and his legacy.

To my mother-in-law Elaine Scott for her grammarian's heart and proofreader's eye.

And thanks to my husband, Bran Scott, who made it possible. Bran is my greatest ally and sincerest love. Between him and God, I've got it made.

GUIDE TO ABBREVIATIONS AND CITATIONS

Abbreviations are used for book citation throughout; articles are named explicitly. Page numbers refer to the book editions cited in the Bibliography. Most citations are to texts easily available in book, journal, or electronic form, rather than to video, audio, and recollected resources which can be difficult to obtain.

Due to copyright limitations, and the challenges in obtaining permissions, some references are provided in abbreviated form. Please note that the beginning and end of a cited passage do not necessarily reflect its content. InterVarsity Press quickly and generously authorized use of all the quotations from *Hearing God*; the rest are used under the Fair Use guidelines of the U.S. Copyright Office.

DC: *The Divine Conspiracy*

GO: *The Great Omission*

HG: *Hearing God*

KCT: *Knowing Christ Today*

RH: *Renovation of the Heart*

SD: *The Spirit of the Disciplines*

Contents

ABIDE

Introduction

Dallas frequently uses the phrase *abide in* in his scriptural paraphrases of the Greek word μένει and its variants, found in the gospel of John and 1 John. The Greek word translates literally as *lives* or *lives in*, but the sense of it is more than simple physical occupation.

When you abide (or dwell) you make a home in the place. You linger, and its reality shapes yours. If you abide in a nonmaterial abode, such as God, or the word, or darkness or light, you are immersed in its real presence: you "inhale" it and it becomes part of you. For example, if you abide in darkness, your inner self will be shaped by the darkness. If you abide in the word of God, your mind fixed on it, your inner self will be shaped by the word, and your whole self will embody its truths. If you abide in God, God's presence will influence and guide your actions.

Notice that abiding in God is not the same thing as obeying God. Obeying God, though important, can be done without your having any real relationship with God. You can also obey God out of fear, or because you were told to. Abiding in God is a relationship of knowledge and trust.

Definition

To abide is to linger in a place, feeling, or nonmaterial substance in such a way that one's inner person is shaped by the abode. To abide in God is to linger in God, allowing one's person to be shaped by God. When one abides in God, one is shaped by the goodness and truth of God, resulting in peace, rest and joy.

Quotes

"Jesus indeed said that without him we can do nothing. (John 15:5) But we can also be sure that if we do nothing it will be without him. So he commands us to abide in the Vine." (15:1-7) We must find a way to do that." (*Living a Transformed Life Adequate to Our Calling*)

"Thus the famous statement of Jesus about truly being his disciples: 'If you abide in my word, then you are truly disciples of mine, and you shall know the truth, and the truth shall make you free.' (John 8:31-32) The 'abiding' here is 'dwelling in' or living in. The word is μείνητε. It is the same basic term used in the great teaching of John 15:1-7 — Abide in me, as the branch dwells in the vine. But what does it mean 'to abide in his word'? It means to put his words into action, to act according to them. When we do that we 'inhale' the reality of the kingdom. That is what it means to be his 'disciples indeed.' And one who does this will come to know the truth, the reality, of the kingdom and of God's action with them, and that in turn will enable them to live free from the bondage of sin." (*Spiritual Formation as a Natural Part of Salvation*)

"Jesus taught us to abide in God's love, 'so that my joy may be in you, and that your joy may be complete.' ... Our joy is complete when there is no room for more. Abiding in God's love provides the unshakable source of joy, which is in turn the source of peace." (GO 129)

Example—Home is a who and a how

We say that a house is not always a home. What is the difference? A house is a physical reality having some set of particular qualities, such as walls, roof, windows, doors, beds, kitchen and so forth. We might argue about what distinguishes a house from an apartment or an office, but it is the physical aspects of the thing that most determine whether it is a house or not.

But while your home could be a house, it might be an apartment, a city, or a family. You may feel at home in an acquaintance's house, and not at home on the street you grew up on. There may be physical qualities that help a place feel like home for you, but ultimately home is not about the what or where of something. It is about who is there, how you experience it, and how it shapes you.

© Wonderlane

The poet Robert Frost wrote "Home is where, when you have to go there, they have to take you in." If you're reading Dallas, you might say that home is where you abide, not where you live.

12

ANGER

Introduction

Your feelings are natural, but they are not always good, and some need to be eliminated or subdued. Anger should be at the top of the list because it is the source of much of the sin in the world. This is because anger is a reaction to someone else's kingdom impinging upon yours. To put it another way, anger comes from having your will thwarted—it is what you feel when you don't get your own way. Anger then moves your will toward interfering or injuring the one who prevented your getting your way. You move to thwart her will, which angers her, impelling her to interfere with or injure you. And so the battle between wills continues.

The other problem with anger is that it cannot be hidden. Its expression varies—contempt, disdain, withdrawal, verbal or physical violence—but it is always expressed. The one at whom the anger is directed is injured, as is anyone who happens to get in the way!

Since anger is a function of the will/spirit/heart, elimination of anger is the first step toward renovation of the heart.

Definition

Anger is the spontaneous feeling that erupts when one's will is thwarted. Anger demands interference or injury, so is always injurious to others.

Quotes

"The primary function of anger in life is to alert me to an obstruction to my will, and immediately raise alarm and resistance, before I even have time to think about it." (DC 148)

"When we trace wrongdoing back to its roots in the human heart, we find that in the overwhelming number of cases it involves some form of anger." (DC 14)

<u>Other relevant citations</u>

DC 147-48: It is a feeling … every degree of anger.

DC 148: Indeed … I am already wounded.

DC 149: Anger … life.

Example – "Righteous" anger?

Think about a time when you were angry at someone. Really angry. Not a little put out or miffed, but actually angry. <u>While you were angry, what</u> did you want? To get your own way, probably, but it's likely you also wanted someone else to *not* have his own way. Even if you could both get what you wanted, while you're angry there is only an either/or, and never a both. It is also pretty likely that you wished the other person harm. Maybe you didn't want grievous bodily harm—we hope you didn't want that!—but the desire to see his plans thwarted, him not to get his way, is wishing a kind of harm.

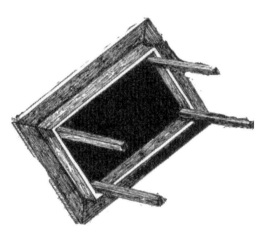

In Matthew 21:12-13, Jesus "drove out" (ἐξέβαλεν) the money changers and merchants. He is usually described as displaying "righteous" anger, because his anger was on God's behalf. By the understanding of anger we are using, was Jesus angry? Can anger be righteous?

<u>Dallas wrote that while we can trust</u> anger and vengeance to God, we cannot trust it to ourselves.

APOLOGETICS

Introduction

Apologetics is the classical term for a systematic, reasoned defense of a viewpoint or idea. When Dallas uses the term, he has a more humble presentation in mind: your explanation of your views and experience given without your intending to intellectually coerce someone else's beliefs. Since the best kind of explanation is example, the best apologetic for Christian belief would be the loving life of a Christian disciple. As a disciple, your life would be a natural extension of your own relationship with Jesus, rather than a means to convince, coerce, or manipulate others into your version of rightness.

Definition

Apologetics is the argument one gives for belief in something. The best apologetics for Christian belief is the transformed life of one of Christ's disciples.

Quotes

"Being mistaken about life and about the things of God and the human soul is a deadly serious matter. That is why the work of apologetics is so important. So we speak the truth in love. (Eph 5:14) And we speak with all the clarity and reasonableness we can muster, simultaneously counting on the Spirit of truth (John 16:13) to accomplish with what we do an effect that lies far beyond our natural abilities." (*Apologetics in the Manner of Jesus*)

"Above all, one has to find by thought and experience that love can be trusted as a way of life. This can be learned by interaction with Jesus in all ordinary and extraordinary circumstances.... Living in love as Jesus defines it by his words and deeds is the sure way to know Christ in the modern world. On the other hand, if you are not reconciled to living in love as the center of your life, and actually living

15

that way, any knowledge you may have of Christ will be shallow and shaky at best." (KCT 93)

Example – The love of saints

A quote widely misattributed to St. Francis of Assisi runs: Preach the gospel always, and if necessary, use words. While Francis never said or wrote this, whoever did was onto something. Who are the saints who populate your life? Perhaps one is the grandfather who always listened. Or maybe a coworker who gently looks homeless beggars in the eye. Those who have the most positive influence on our lives rarely do it just with words: something about them speaks loudly before their words ever do. That something is love, which is the only real apologetic Christian faith ever needs.

©Grzegorz Łobiński

APPRENTICE

Introduction

This is a primary Willardian word, appearing in *Renovation of the Heart* alone 59 times! Throughout his Christian work, Dallas uses the word *apprentice* for those who arrange their daily lives around following Jesus. He also uses the more common word *disciple*, but prefers *apprentice* because in contemporary conversation *disciple* is frequently used as a synonym for *believer*. That would be fine, except that *believer* has come to designate anyone who is willing to assent to a particular statement *about* Jesus, whether doing so affects their daily lives or not.

The goal of apprenticeship is not to behave like Jesus, but to develop a heart that has been transformed through effort and grace to be like Jesus'. A person with a transformed heart easily obeys God, thus routinely doing everything Jesus says is best and abiding in the grace and joy of God.

Apprentices to Jesus are those who intentionally and persistently learn to live their lives as Jesus would live them were he they. They learn from Jesus how to be like Jesus, just as a medieval apprentice would have lived with his master, doing what he did, learning the daily skills and ways of thinking that made the master good at what he did. It was the constant attention to the way of the master that helped the apprentice become like him. So it is with apprentices to Jesus. The more mature the apprentice, the more the influence of the master affects everything. So a banker who is an apprentice will abide with Jesus while banking, living the banking life as Jesus would live his banking life if he were the banker. That is the behavior piece: behaving like Jesus because your heart is like his. The person with the renovated heart cannot help but include God in every aspect of life.

[Definition follows on next page.]

17

Definition

An apprentice (*or* disciple) is one who is intentionally and persistently learning to live his or her own life as Jesus would live it if it were his. The result of apprenticeship is easy and routine obedience to God, doing what Jesus said to do and did.

Quotes

"[To be an apprentice] is to be one of those who have trusted Jesus with their whole life, so far as they understand it. Because they have done so they want to learn everything he has to teach them about life in the kingdom of God now and forever, and they are constantly with him to learn this. Disciples of Jesus are those who are with him learning to be like him. That is, they are learning to lead their life, their actual existence, as he would lead their life if he were they. This is what they are learning together in their local gatherings, and with those gatherings a constant part of their life, they are learning how to walk with Jesus and learn from him in every aspect of their individual lives." (RH 241)

"[To] be someone's apprentice, there is one absolutely essential condition. I must be with that person …. And provision has been made for us to be with Jesus, as one person to another, in our daily life. But it is also necessary that we have a practical … understanding of this arrangement in order to carry on our side of the apprenticeship relation." (DC 276)

Other relevant citations

KCT 54: As Jesus's disciple … Yes, the very life you have.

RH 231: [The call of Christ] is … everything he said.

Example – The plumber

In her book, *When the Soul Listens*, Dallas' longtime collaborator and student Jan Johnson quotes one of Dallas' examples of living as an apprentice in real life. Notice the connection Dallas makes between abiding and apprenticing.

Photographer unknown

"Let's say I'm a plumber and I'm going to clean out someone's sewer. How will I do this as Jesus would do it? If you encounter difficulties with the people you're serving or with the pipe or the machinery, you never fight that battle alone. You invoke the presence of God. You expect to see something happen that is not the result of you ….

The crucial thing is to be attentive to God's hand, not to get locked into one-on-one thinking: It's me and this pipe! Never do that. A person has to train himself to think, Now is the time to rely on God and to praise him for the solution that will come to me. That's called 'life in God.' Training brings you to the point where you don't have to say, 'I have to pay attention!' You routinely think, This is an occasion when God is present." (Dallas Willard, quoted by Jan Johnson in her book *When the Soul Listens*, page 145)

BELIEF

Introduction

We tend to think of belief as a lesser form of knowledge. Where knowledge is an idea that is true or could be proven true, belief seems to be something we hope (or fear) is true without having proof. That is, in common usage a "belief" is a just an idea we do not know to be true.

In Dallas' work, belief is a different type of idea than knowledge. Beliefs may turn out to be true or false, but what matters about them is that they that motivate our actions. Beliefs have a connection to the will—to our actions and behavior—that knowledge does not. You can know something and take no action on your knowledge. If you actually believe something, you are prepared to act on that belief. When beliefs are founded in knowledge, they are reliable guides to behavior. When they are founded on emotion or falsehoods, they may be true, but are not consistently reliable.

What makes this trickier is that we are not always aware of our real beliefs; in fact most of what we believe we never even think about. And, judging by our actions, we often believe ideas that, if asked, we would say were false!

Definition

A belief is an idea on which we are prepared to take action. Beliefs are motivating factors in our lives; they are the ideas that move the will.

Quotes

"Belief is when your whole being is set to act as if something is so."(RH 248)

"*Belief*, by contrast [to knowledge], has no necessary tie to truth, good method, or evidence … . In its basic nature belief is a matter of *tendencies to act* … to believe something involves a readiness to act, in

21

appropriate circumstances, *as if* what is believed were so. Thus belief involves the will in a way that knowledge does not." (KCT 16)

Other relevant citations

DC 318: To believe … so.

KCT 19: Ideally, knowledge … it is mere profession.

Example – The non-discovery of America

In 1492 the rulers of Spain granted Christopher Columbus the backing to journey to the East Indies by sailing westward. As is well known, he missed the East Indies by about 10,000 miles, landing in what is now known as the Bahamas. Clearly Columbus did not know where he was going, but believed he would wind up where he wanted to go. On the other hand, you might very well know all about both the East Indies and the Bahamas, including their locations, yet have no inclination to go to either one.

Example – Belief about vs. belief in

We are often encouraged to believe something *about* Jesus, such as that he is the messiah, that he never sinned, lived in a particular place and time and so forth. When we believe *about* we are mostly agreeing that some claim is true. However, believing *in* Jesus is about trusting *him*, and being ready with our whole person to act as if what he says is so.

Imagine a child standing at the edge of a pool, legs shivering, afraid to jump to his mother who is standing in the water. He doesn't jump because even if he knows it's safe, he doesn't believe it. If the child jumps to his mother, it won't be because he believes something about water and depth and drowning, but because he believes in—trusts— his mother. The child's belief in his mother is what impels him to jump.

THE BIBLE, ASSUMPTIONS ABOUT

Introduction

~~Dallas' deep respect for and knowledge of the Bible shines through every aspect of his thinking~~. It is his vast, considered, and lived understanding of Scripture that founds his work. These are his operating assumptions about the Bible; quotes supporting each assumption are listed by number.

1. The Bible is a sacred communication through which God is revealed and actively self-reveals.

2. The Bible is a reliable and realistic treatise on a life lived well, that is, in accordance with the principles outlined in Scripture and lived out by Jesus.

3. Though the Bible is inerrant in the original, we are not, and our collations, translations, and interpretations should be approached with the ultimate humility.

4. Bible memorization is the critical discipline.

Quotes

1. The Bible is a sacred communication through which God is revealed and actively self-reveals.

"Scripture is a *communication* that establishes *communion* and opens the way to *union*, all is a way that is perfectly understandable once we begin to have experience of it." (HG 161)

2. The Bible is a reliable and realistic treatise on a life lived well, that is, in accordance with the principles outlined in Scripture and lived out by Jesus.

"How do such Bible stories [about transformation] help? Upon a realistic, critical, adult reading, by those prepared to be honest with their experience, the Bible incisively lays bare the depths and obscurities of the human heart ... [I]t is fitted to be the perpetual instrument of the Spirit of God for human transformation ... . But the

23

Bible also informs us that there are certain *practices*—solitude, prayer, fasting, celebration, and so forth—we can undertake, in cooperation with grace, to raise the level of our lives toward godliness." (SD 69)

"[A] biblical Christian is not just someone who holds certain beliefs *about* the Bible. He or she is also someone who *leads the kind of life demonstrated* in the Bible: a life of personal, intelligent interaction with God." (HG 103)

3.   Though the original form of the Bible is inerrant, we are not, and our collations, translations, and interpretations should be approached with the ultimate humility.

"The Bible is one of the results of God's speaking. It is the unique written Word of God. It is inerrant in its original form and infallible in all of its forms for the purpose of guiding us into a life-saving relationship with God in his kingdom. It is infallible in this way precisely because God never leaves it alone .... The inerrancy of the original texts is rendered effective for the purposes of redemption only as that text, through its present-day derivatives, is constantly held within the eternal living Word ... Inerrancy of the originals also does not guarantee sane and sound, much less error-free, interpretation. Our dependence as we read the Bible today must be on God, who now speaks to us in conjunction with it and with our best efforts to understand it." (HG 141-42)

"We will be spiritually safe in our use of the Bible if we follow a simple rule: *Read with a submissive attitude*... Subordinate your desire to *find* the truth to your desire to *do* it, to act it out!" (HG 161)

4.   Bible memorization is the critical discipline.

"Bible memorization is absolutely fundamental to spiritual formation. If I had to—and of course I don't have to—choose between all the disciplines of the spiritual life and take only one, I would choose Bible memorization." (GO 58)

24

Other relevant citations

DC xvi: On the human side …. On the divine side … into life in God's kingdom.

GO 126: This practice … the entirety of our lives.

GO 172: Christians who do read their Bibles … transformation of our lives.

RH 197: Spiritual formation in Christ … presented as the truth.

BLESSING

Introduction

At the last session of the inaugural conference of the Dallas Willard Center (February 23, 2013), Dallas led the four hundred gathered apprentices through an exercise of blessing. It was an exposition of the blessing of Numbers 6:24-26, followed by an uncharacteristic exercise: in pairs the attendees slowly blessed each other, then as a group blessed Dallas, using the blessing. Though unusual, it was a fitting and generous end to his last public appearance.

The following is excerpted and adapted from that talk.

Sharing Blessing

Blessing is the projection of good into the life of another, as cursing is the projection of evil. It is putting forth your will for the good of another person. You bless someone when you will their good under the invocation of God. True blessing always involves God.

As Christ's apprentices, we want to be points of constant blessing moving out to the world beyond us. We are to be engaged in blessing throughout our lives. We are to bless, and curse not.

Blessing is a generous outpouring of our whole being. It is a profoundly personal act. It cannot be hurried: we want to be able to put our whole self into it.

Blessing requires getting the other person to hold still long enough to receive. We have to learn to receive blessing. It is our habit to deflect the blessing, particularly by thinking about how and when to bless them back even as they are blessing us! But blessing is an act of grace, not of indebtedness.

The great blessing of Numbers 6:24-26 is a good one to use. It is hard to improve upon one that God gave and commanded its use. When you bless someone, slow down and think about what you are

27

saying. Picture his or her face; hold the person before your mind and your heart. Pour out your heart for their good upon him or her.

May God bless you and keep you. The "you" here is important; underline the "you": May God bless you and keep you. God bring good constantly into your life—that is what blessing is. God keep you safely, in the power of the blood of Jesus.

God make his face to shine upon you. If it is hard for you to imagine the shining face of God, think about a doting grandparent when the grandchild appears. The grandparent's face shines. It is radiant. "God make his face to shine upon you" is "may you live before the shining face of God, God's radiant face, spilling out glory." Glory is meant to be shared, from God through us to others.

The Lord be gracious unto you. May the flow of his love and creating nature be on you.

The Lord lift up his countenance upon you. May the Lord look right at you personally. We know God is everywhere all the time, but God is not manifest everywhere. May the manifest presence of God be there with you.

And give you peace, which comes only in the presence of God. We are asking for an entire atmosphere of God's blessing, for the person we are blessing to live in the atmosphere of peace and blessing. The transformed person generates an atmosphere of blessing.

We are to be, and shall be, a community of persons of overflowing blessing. As an apprentice, say to yourself, "I am a person of blessing."

BODY

Introduction

Since the ancient Greeks, Western people have tended to think of themselves as having two completely separate parts: the physical part (your body) and the nonphysical part (your soul or mind or spirit). This division is responsible for all manner of philosophical questions, but the one that has cut across science, government, ethics—all areas of human thinking—is this: which is the *real* person, the body or the soul/mind/spirit?

Dallas did not accept this dichotomy. Instead he suggested that the human person or self actually has five essential dimensions: body, soul, social environment, mind (both thoughts and feelings), and spirit (also called "will" or "heart"). This means we are not essentially souls or spirits who happen to be lodging *in* bodies, nor are we really just physical collections of chemicals and electrical charges. The body is the physical part of what makes up our self.

When Dallas used the word *body* he had in mind at least four characteristics of bodies:

1. The body is one of five essential dimensions of the self.

2. The body is the physical aspect of a person, and is the repository of our actions, habits, and character. Its use also shapes our actions, habits, and character: it is the locus of our spiritual formation.

3. The body is the source of power and of energy.

4. The body is essentially social, not private, as it is the interface between us and the rest of creation.

These characteristics come together in a passage from Spirit of the Disciplines:

"[W]e alone among living beings can stand in opposition to God—in order that we may also choose to stand *with* God … The human body itself then is part of the *imago Dei*, for it is the vehicle through which we can affectively acquire the limited self-

29

subsistent power we must have to be truly in the image and likeness of God … . In creating human beings in his likeness so that we could govern in his manner, God gave us a measure of *independent* power. Without such power, we absolutely could not resemble God in the close manner he intended, nor could we be God's co-workers. *The locus or depository of this necessary power is the human body.* This explains, in theological terms, why we have a body at all. *That body is our primary area of power, freedom, and—therefore—responsibility.* (SD 52-53)

Definition

The body is the physical aspect of the human person and the locus of the activity of spiritual formation. It is the source of our power in and our interface with the physical world.

Quotes

1.   The body is one of five essential dimensions of the self.

(*See* Six (or Five) Aspects of the Human Person *for applicable quotes.*)

2.   The body is the physical aspect of a person, and is the repository of our actions, habits, and character. Its use also shapes our actions, habits, and character: it is the locus of our spiritual formation.

   "Learning Christ-likeness is not passive. It is active engagement with and in God. And we act with our bodies. Moreover, this bodily engagement is what lays the foundation in our bodily members for readinesses for holiness, and increasingly removes the readinesses to sin … " (GO 90)

   "The proper retraining and nurturing of the body is absolutely essential to Christlikeness. The body is not just a physical thing. As it matures, it increasingly takes on the quality of 'inner' life." (RH 165)

3.   The body is the source of power and of energy.

   "The body is the focal point of our presence in the physical and social world. In union with it we come into existence, and we become the person we shall forever be. It is our primary energy source or "strength"—our personalized 'power pack'." (RH 35)

4.   The body is essentially social, not private, as it is the interface between us and the rest of creation.

"Human personal relations cannot be separated from the body; and, on the other hand, the body cannot be understood apart from human relations. It is essentially social …. Our choices, as they settle into character (to be explained later) are "farmed out" or "outsourced" to our body in its social context, where they then occur more or less "automatically," without our having to think about what we are doing." (RH 35)

Other relevant citations

DC 353-54: [T]he body is the first field of energy …. resource for the spiritual life.

RH 160: I can only liberate and use … extend our "kingdom."

RH 166: These various tendencies … The tongue, for example.

RH 169: Because we are essentially … with as I will.

RH 170: [An apprentice's] body … "a showplace of God's greatness."

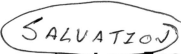

BORN AGAIN (OR LIFE FROM ABOVE)

Introduction

Dallas preferred the term *life from above* partly because it skirts the commonly understood meaning of *born again*. The phrase *born again* has come to indicate a personal status in which one has been forgiven by God and is destined for an everlasting life in heaven. The phrase tends to be used to refer to the moment of choice, the "yes" of salvation, that marks your new chance at a better life. So the statement "I have been born again" tends to be seen as equivalent to "I have been saved." This thin notion suggests that getting into heaven is the point of salvation and that transformation of the inner person is an add-on.

But the fact of being born again is richer than that. At justification (the first step of salvation), you receive a life—an additional life—that regenerates your soul and allows for the Spirit of God to work in and through you in the work of transformation. Regeneration is, as Jesus says in John 3:3, what allows someone to "see" (participate in) the Kingdom of God. So being born again is not just another way of referring to your ticket to heaven; it is what happens when you receive the actual new life of Christ from above that allows you to have a new life in Christ here below.

Definition

To be born again is to gain the life from above, enabling an interactive life with God and God's kingdom.

Quotes

"We have to deal with a massive population of churched and unchurched people who think of 'being saved' or 'being right with God' merely in terms of some picture of justification, not regeneration. Being 'born again' is usually understood now, not in terms of being animated by a 'life from above,' but in terms of a profession of faith—often a profession of faith in the death of Christ

33

as bearing the punishment for sin that otherwise would fall on us. This understanding usually prevails in ways that do not involve—may not even make mention of—participation in divine life. (And, of course, one can mention it without engaging it.) Then, of course, the otherwise natural progression into discipleship and its spiritual (trans)formation *naturally* does *not* occur, and the churches and surrounding society is flooded with discipleshipless Christians whose lives seem not to differ profoundly, if at all, from non-Christians." (*Spiritual Formation as a Natural Part of Salvation*)

"Our additional life, though it is still our life, is also God's life in us: his thoughts, his faith, his love, all *literally* imparted to us, shared with us, by his word and Spirit." (HG 157)

Other relevant citations

DC 68: [The "birth from above" literally is] the receiving of a superhuman kind of life … "The Kingdom Among Us."

DC 198: In John 3 … new start in life.

Introduction

Obeying laws requires effort. You have to pay attention to the speed limit, your speedometer, and your impatience. You have to resist putting batteries into the recycling bin. The season's first strawberries at the grocery store seem to long to be sampled, and you have to reason with yourself in order to not snitch one. Most of us try to obey laws through mental gymnastics or force of will. But force of will alone will not keep the habits of our bodies and mind in check. That means that we cannot hope to unfailingly keep the law just by keeping the law.

You may have noticed that the best law-keepers are not necessarily the best people. Obeying laws alone does not lead us to be the kind of people God intends us to be. If we keep the law by force of will, we will fail. And if we see obeying the law as the ultimate faithfulness, we will become lawkeepers instead of people in relationship with God and each other. To consistently keep the law (or do God's will, or to live under God's reign) while being good people, we must become the kind of people who do the right thing automatically. And that is determined by our character.

Your character is made up of your accumulated beliefs and behavioral inclinations, or what Dallas called your *settled dispositions*. It largely determines your responses and behaviors. That is, in any given set of circumstances, you are more likely to behave *this* way rather than *that* because of your character. Character takes over when you are not thinking, and often when you are. To consistently do what Jesus did—the right thing—automatically, your character needs to be like his. That is the focus of Christian spiritual formation: transforming your character to be like Christ's through the grace and power of God coupled with your action and intention. Transform your character and obedience becomes nearly effortless.

Definition

One's character is the largely fixed accumulation of beliefs, and inclinations to behave in certain ways in particular circumstances. One's character ultimately determines one's choice sets and one's actions. To consistently act like Jesus requires a character like his. Thus the transformation of one's character to be more like Christ's is the disciple's goal, achieved through the grace and power of God coupled with one's action and intention.

Quotes

1.   One's character is the largely fixed accumulation of beliefs, and inclinations to behave in certain ways in particular circumstances. One's character ultimately determines one's choice sets and one's actions.

"'Character' refers to the settled dispositions to act in certain ways, given the relevant circumstances. Character is expressed in what one does without thinking, as well as to what one does after acting without thinking. The actions which come from character will usually persist when the individual is unobserved, as well as when the consequences of the action are not what one would prefer. A person of good moral character is one who, from the deeper and more pervasive dimensions of the self, is intent upon advancing the various goods of human life with which they are effectively in contact (etc.)." (*Why It Matters If You Are Moral*)

2.   To consistently act like Jesus requires a character like his. The transformation of one's character to be more like Christ's is the disciple's goal, and is achieved through the grace and power of God coupled with our action and intention.

"[We] must learn from Jesus, our 'in-former,' a new internal character." (GO 21)

36

"Character is formed through action, and it is transformed through action, including carefully planned and grace-sustained disciplines." (GO 65)

<u>Other relevant citations</u>

DC 142-43: [We] cannot keep the law by trying ... naturally flow.

RH 19: We each become ... specific type of character.

RH 142: Our character is ... automatically arise.

RH 142: [Character] can be changed ... is about.

RH 144: [Will] is not the same thing ... give rise to character.

RH 251: The renovation of the heart ... key.

Example – Gyges' ring

In *The Republic* the philosopher Plato poses an ethical question: would an intelligent, sane person behave morally if one knew one would not be caught. His character Glaucon—a cynical sort— responds with a thought experiment based on a legend.

A shepherd named Gyges served the king of Lydia. During a great storm, an earthquake opened the earth in front of him. Gyges entered the opening and discovered a number of astonishing things, including a gold ring which he took. At a meeting of shepherds Gyges is fiddling with his ring, when suddenly he becomes invisible. His fellow shepherds even speak of him as if he were not there. Gyges uses the power of the ring to seduce the queen of Lydia, slay the king, and take the kingdom.

Glaucon proposed the idea of two such rings, suggesting that if a just man wore one and an unjust man the other, both would steal what they could, lie when they could, kill as they desired. Glaucon's idea was that it is only fear of punishment that makes for so-called just action.

Socrates responded that the just man would not use the ring, because unlike the unjust one, the just man is not enslaved by his appetites. Because the just man had self-control, he would be happy even without the material and social benefits of the ring.

The similarities between Dallas' emphasis on character development, though founded on the work of Plato's student Aristotle, and the view belonging to Plato's rendition of Socrates should be clear. For both, if one gets to the point of being tempted and thinks one can get away with it, one will choose to act unjustly (or at least will have a hard time choosing not to do so). It is up to the individual to tame the appetites (or subdue the flesh) so that he or she is able to act justly, which provides greater happiness (or joy) than acquisition of social and material goods.

CHILDREN OF LIGHT

Introduction

In chapter 12 of *Renovation of the Heart* Dallas compellingly uses the biblical term *children of light* to refer to those people who hearts have been transformed through the power of God and their own activity. In classical terms, the children of light are those who have been justified and are being sanctified. Through regeneration their nature is like that of Christ, who is light. Through their sanctification their souls have been restored to wholeness, and are at home in God: the light of Christ shines through them.

The children of light are the true saints of God. They are what Jesus' apprentices aspire to be.

Definition

The children of light are people whose hearts have been transformed into Christlikeness. Having developed the character of Christ, they consistently and automatically participate in active fellowship with God, doing what Jesus would do were he living their lives.

Quotes

"To call them *children* of light is, in biblical terminology, to say that they have the basic nature of light: that light is their parent and has passed on to them its nature, as any parent does." (RH 218)

Other relevant citations

RH 141: [What those renovated in Christlikeness look like.] We know that they will … faith and hope.

RH 219-20: Their body has come over to the side … strength that is from God.

RH 227: [The marks of those who have become established in their whole being as children of light.] One is that … in human relations as well as before God.

CONFESSION

Introduction

As one of the classical, time-tested disciplines, confession is an important piece of the disciple's plan for spiritual transformation. It is also a sacred trust in the community of believers: there can be no beloved community without the twin disciplines of confession and fellowship.

Definition

Confession is the activity of humble transparency: sharing our deepest weaknesses, failures, beliefs, and burdens with one or more trusted others. Confession is admitting to the condition of your soul.

Quotes

"These means [of transformation are] primarily, the disciplines for life in the Spirit: solitude and silence, prayer and fasting, worship and study, fellowship and confession, and the like." (GO 74)

"Confession is a discipline that functions within fellowship. In it we let trusted others know our deepest weaknesses and failures. This will nourish our faith in God's provision for our needs through his people, our sense of being loved, and our humility before our brothers and sisters. Thus we let some friends in Christ know who we really are, not holding back anything important but, ideally, allowing complete transparency. We lay down the burden of hiding and pretending, which normally takes up such a dreadful amount of human energy. We engage and are engaged by others in the most profound depths of the soul … . Confession alone makes *deep* fellowship possible, and the lack of it explains much of the superficial quality so commonly found in our church associations. What, though, makes confession bearable? Fellowship. There is an essential reciprocity between these two disciplines…" (SD 187-89)

Example – You don't have to get drunk

Confession may be the hardest spiritual discipline, at least if you're doing it right. Most of us confess our sins or weakness under one of four circumstances: 1) as part of a formal liturgy, 2) when we are so burdened by guilt that we dump it on someone else – usually the person we've harmed, 3) when we're drunk and blithering, or 4) when we're not drunk anymore and are on the 5th step of the 12-step program.

©Pedro Ribeiro Simões

Truth be told, we generally don't confess everything even when we think we do: we hold back out of fear, pride, or shame. Sometimes we're afraid of others' reaction, including God's. Sometimes we are prideful and don't want to admit how weak we really are. Sometimes—even most of the time—we don't really share deeply because we are ashamed to even look at our hearts, never mind telling others what is there. That combination of fear, pride, and shame is deadly to spiritual development, because it traps us into thinking that we are enough, and alone.

Throughout his work, Dallas emphasizes the communal nature of confession. For the practice to be successful you have to be among people you trust, starting with God and yourself. With others, this comes with a mutual vulnerability, a shared humility. To look deeply at our selves requires that we have the unshakable belief that we are loved by God, and there is nothing that can change that. Nothing we have done earns God's love, and nothing we have done destroys it. God's love—not booze or bravado—is what can give us the confidence to examine ourselves honestly and openly.

CONTEMPT

Introduction

With anger, contempt is the most common root of wrongdoing. Contempt is the degrading response to others that excludes them from one's own little world. Contempt renders its object irrelevant, destroying both belonging and fellowship, which are among the deepest needs of human beings. It rejects the value of another person, though that person is equally beloved of God. Such degradation and exclusion is anathema to the reign of God and the character of Christ, so disciples must root it out of their lives.

One cannot overstate the importance Dallas placed on eliminating contempt from one's thoughts and character.

Definition

Contempt is a mixture of disdain and disgust, derived from anger and degrading to others. Its object is thus rejected and dishonored, put out of community and relationship.

Quotes

"[Contempt is a kind of] studied degradation of another." (DC 151)

"In anger I want to hurt you. In contempt, I don't care whether you are hurt or not." (DC 151)

Other relevant citations

DC 147: When we trace wrongdoing … step toward the rightness of the kingdom heart.

DC 152: The intent and the effect of contempt … made fair game for worse treatment.

DC 153: To belong is a vital need … destroy so deeply that murder would almost be a mercy.

DEATH TO SELF (OR SELF-DENIAL)

Introduction

Death to self is the goal of self-denial.

Self-denial is simply laying down the burden of having your own way. It is not denying that you have a self – that you are an individual person – but refraining from satisfying its whims. As Dallas puts it, to deny oneself is to "reject the preeminence of what we want, when and as we want it." (RH 71)

Self-denial is not self-hatred or contempt: you do not lose value or integrity by denying yourself. Rather, self-denial breaks the tyranny of desire's power over your will, allowing love of God and neighbor to reign over your thoughts and behaviors. When you don't have to get what you want in order to be happy or fulfilled or right, you discover that what you want is not so important after all. Therefore, self-denial—not punishment or self-abuse—is the basis of Christian spiritual formation. Death to self is what allows Christ to be fully alive in you.

Definition

Death to self is the result of self-denial. It is the state of tender indifference to the outcries of one's desires, with the attendant elimination of their power over one's will, in which one is freed to worship and enjoy God now and eternally.

Quotes

"Being dead to self is the condition where the mere fact that I do not get what I want does not surprise or offend me and has no control over me." (RH 71)

Other relevant citations

RH 68: So the self-denial of Matthew 16: 24 … creating you.

RH 71: At the first we must ... and willing are wrongly poised [toward self-worship].

RH 73: [T]hose who are dead to self ... no longer are locked in a struggle with it.

See also John Calvin, *Institutes of Religion*, book three chapters 7 and 8.

Example—Death to self and martyrdom

We have all known people who have no self-interest. Or that's

You are here

what they say when they tell us they really don't mind loading up our moving van for the third time this year. In churches they are often so busy with committees, service, and programs that we wonder how anything could run without them. In families they are the ones who won't say they want Thai food then feel vaguely resentful when we go for Mexican.

In much the same way that humility is not the same as humiliation, self-denial is nothing like being a martyr. When you deny your self, you're not saying you don't matter. You're saying that you are not the center of the universe. Over time, as you gently but repeatedly practice not getting what you want, what you want loosens its grip on you. Your desire for control over a project or your environment fades. It's not that you stop caring, or that you allow yourself to be abused. Instead, your self becomes part of the whole picture, rather than the reference point. The pain that comes from a slight or offense turns from a stab in the back to a stubbed toe.

As you come out of the center of your universe, God can take your place there. The universe itself becomes a much more benign — even joyful — place to live.

DECISION MAKING

Introduction

Dallas put tremendous emphasis on our ability to think, reason, and choose. More than once he stated that our primary freedom as human beings is where to place our mind. Our mind is the source of our feelings and thoughts, but it is also the locus of decision. Though decision affects the actions of the will, decision itself is a function of the mind. Decisions come out of your character and effect action, which in turn shapes character. So, what you are doing with your mind at any given point will guide or determine your decisions and shape your character.

Dallas used the language of decision and of *settled intent* interchangeably; by definition a decision requires that one's intention be settled. That is, if you have an intent, and it is truly settled in you, decision happens. For Dallas, deciding entails acting, so if one doesn't act one didn't actually decide. If you claim to have a goal, and do not take appropriate action to achieve it, you did not decide to reach the goal, which means your intent to reach it was never "settled." If intention is "settled," decision happens and action occurs.

In *The Divine Conspiracy* Dallas notes that the heart of relationship is asking the other to do or give something: by asking (rather than assuming or coercing, for example) you acknowledge the other's freedom, and value and grant the power of decision. Thus decision, and our ability to decide, is key to human interaction with God, self, and others.

Definition

Decision is the activity of the mind that motivates the will to action and shapes character. It automatically derives from a settled intention to do or achieve something and completes that intention.

47

Quotes

1.   Decision is the activity of the mind that motivates the will to action and shapes character.

"Now, an intention is whole and real only if it includes a decision to fulfill or carry through with the intention. We commonly find people who say they intend (or intended) to do certain things that they do not do. To be fair, external circumstances may sometimes have prevented them from carrying out the action. And habits deeply rooted in our bodies and life contexts can, for a while, thwart even a sincere intention. But if something like that is not the case, we know that they never actually decided to do what they say they intended to do, and that they therefore did not really intend to do it." *(Living a Transformed Life Adequate to Our Calling)*

2.   It automatically derives from a settled intention to do or achieve something and completes that intention.

"In the heart of the disciple there is a desire, and there is decision or settled intent ... .Given this desire, usually produced by the lives and words of those already in The Way, there is yet a decision to be made: the decision to devote oneself to becoming like Christ." (SD 263)

Other relevant citations

RH 30: [There are] six basic aspects ... choice (will, decision, character).

RH 89: Here the means in question ... decisions, and character.

Example—Healthy lifestyle

Around midnight on December 31st a lot of people discover a desire to live a healthier lifestyle. On January 1st, a good number of those people enroll in health clubs. On January 2nd, health clubs are packed. By February 1st, health club parking lots across the land are once again nearly vacant. What happened to all those New Year's good intentions?

48

Here is a more Willardian way to read this set of events.

Around midnight on December 31st a lot of people discover their desire to live a healthier lifestyle, and have the intention of doing so. On January 1st, a good number of those people still have the desire and the intention, and so take action by enrolling in health clubs. As time passes, those whose intention is settled—who had really resolved and decided—continue to take action. Others whose intention is not settled stop taking action: they had never really decided to live a healthier lifestyle. Others decided to take action, but circumstances prevented their following through on the intention.

For those of us who have the desire, have settled intentions, and still have to "decide" every day whether to go to the gym, it is the inertia of the flesh that threatens to unsettle the intention. It's not that we have to keep deciding, though it feels like that, but that our minds and bodies and wills have to deal with the habits of the flesh.

DISCIPLE

Introduction

Most any dictionary will tell you that a disciple is someone who accepts and adheres to the doctrine or teaching of another. The problem with this definition is that it seems to express a mental state only: accepting. Even adhering requires no activity that isn't explicitly demanded. Under this intellectual definition of disciple, one could accept a teaching, be devoted to its truth, even profess belief in it without actually *doing* anything about it.

Dallas preferred the word *apprentice* since it suggests activity, particularly activity done in emulation of an expert for the purpose of becoming like the expert in some significant way. Certainly Jesus' original disciples operated as apprentices, as he intended when he said, "I tell you the truth, anyone who has faith in me will do what I have been doing. He will do even greater things than these" (John 14:12, NIV). But disciple is the more common word; when Dallas used it he intended a far richer meaning than mere mental assent.

> ## Definition
>
> A disciple of Jesus is someone who 1) trusts Jesus, and that he is who and what he says he is, 2) spends time with Jesus in order to learn how to live his or her own life as Jesus would live it were Jesus the disciple, and 3) rearranges his or her life in order to keep doing that.

Quotes

1. A disciple trusts Jesus, and that he is who and what he says he is.

   "[The] gospel of the entire New Testament is that you can have new life now in the Kingdom of God if you will trust Jesus Christ. Not just something he did, or something he said, but trust the whole person of Christ in everything he touches—which is everything." (GO 61)

2.   A disciple spends time with Jesus in order to learn how to live his or her own life as Jesus would live it if Jesus were the disciple.

"[A] disciple, or apprentice, is simply someone who has decided to be with another person, under appropriate conditions, in order to become capable of doing what that person does or to become what that person is …. And as a disciple of Jesus I am with him, by choice and by grace, learning from him how to live in the kingdom of God … how to live within the range of God's effective will, his life flowing through mine … I am learning from Jesus to live my life as he would live my life if he were I. I am not necessarily learning to do everything he did, but I am learning how to do everything I do in the manner that he did all that he did … .I am learning from Jesus how to lead my life, my whole life, my real life …" (DC 282-84)

3.   A disciple rearranges his or her life in order to keep being with and learning from Jesus.

"The disciple is one who, intent upon becoming Christ-like and so dwelling in his "faith and practice," systematically and progressively rearranges his affairs to that end." (GO 7)

Other relevant citations

DC 291: In summary … rearranging their affairs—to do this.

DC 318: Jesus' disciples … to be like him.

GO 14: You can't trust him … every aspect of your life.

GO 16: Our aim is to be pervasively possessed by Jesus through constant companionship with him.

RH 87: Concretely, we intend … trust in him takes.

Example—Democracy

Imagine an American who accepts democracy as the only proper form of government, defends it wholeheartedly, reads books and treatises about it, and even goes so far as to have a portrait of Thomas Jefferson hanging prominently on the living room wall. The American is a disciple of democracy, perhaps of Thomas Jefferson as well. Does it take any stretch of your imagination to picture that same person not voting, or not exercising some other right or responsibility associated with democracy? Probably not. This is the problem with the word *disciple* as it is currently used: it is all about thinking and almost nothing about doing.

In July 2013, Eugene Cho tweeted: "Discipleship isn't a class you take after becoming a follower of Christ. To follow Christ IS to be a disciple of Christ." We couldn't have said it better ourselves.

 S̶e̶l̶f̶— DISCIPLINE(S)

Introduction

Your behaviors and abilities are lodged in your body. No matter if they are mental or physical, behaviors, abilities, and even identity reside in your body. If you want to change a behavior or improve an ability, you have to use your body in a planful, systematic way.

Orderly and systematic activities intended to change a behavior or improve an ability are called *disciplines*. They are almost always indirect; that is, disciplines work on the habits and skills of mind and body that enable the larger goal. "A discipline is any activity within our power that we engage in to enable us to do what we cannot do by direct effort" (*Living a Transformed Life Adequate to Our Calling*). We use disciplines to retrain our bodies and minds into patterns of activity that enable us to do what we want to do. Disciplines work because they mold and shape the embodied self.

Notice that the desired habit or ability is not itself a discipline; the orderly and systematic activities that lead to the habit or ability are the disciplines. Playing the piano is not a discipline; practice is. Disciplines have no purpose in themselves other than to lead to the desired behavior or ability. When a discipline becomes a point of pride or a basis for self-righteousness, it loses its value.

Discipline (sometimes called *self-discipline*) also refers to the character trait needed to achieve a significant or long-term goal, or to act when acting is right. Discipline is what makes it possible for you to do what needs to be done when and how it needs to be done. To develop the character trait of discipline you need the activity of disciplines.

Definition

Discipline is a character trait formed by and expressed through the body that enables a person to do what needs to be done when and how it needs to be done.

A discipline is any activity pursued in an orderly and systematic manner that improves or determines other activities, including our habits and abilities.

Quotes

1. Discipline is a character trait formed by and expressed through activities of the body that enables a person to do what needs to be done when and how it needs to be done.

   "Discipline is in fact a natural part of the structure of the human soul, and almost nothing of any significance in education, culture, or other attainments is achieved without it. Everything from learning a language to weight-lifting depends upon it, and its availability in the human makeup is what makes the individual human being responsible for the kind of person he or she becomes." (GO 151)

2. A discipline is any activity pursued in an orderly and systematic manner that improves or determines other activities, including our habits and abilities.

   "A discipline is any activity within our power that we engage in to enable us to do what we cannot do by direct effort ... Practice is discipline, but not all discipline is practice, for in many disciplines we do not engage in the very activity that we hope to be good at ... simple sleep and rest may be disciplines in the sense just described. They will, as we have said, enable us to do what we cannot do by direct effort, including staying in good emotional and physical health ... But usually when we rest we would not be practicing resting." (DC 353)

   Other relevant citations

   DC 355: [The] disciplined person ... needs to be done.

56

SD 92-93: [The role of disciplines] rests upon … and *shape it.*

SD 120: Discipline … but to play it well.

See also Aristotle's *Nicomachean Ethics.*

"It is well said, then, that it is by doing just acts that the just man is produced, and by doing temperate acts the temperate man; without doing these no one would have even a prospect of becoming good." (Aristotle, *Nicomachean Ethics,* 1105b, 10-12)

"We are inquiring, not in order to know what virtue is, but in order to become good, since otherwise our inquiry would have been of no use." (Aristotle, *Nicomachean Ethics,* 1103b, 27-30)

Example – Playing the piano

To use Dallas' example, if you want to be a pianist, you have to use your body and mind in particular ways, regularly and systematically, to engage with the piano. You won't become a competent pianist by playing the piano. You have to practice the skills, training your body and mind into the habits of activity and thinking that make piano playing possible. Practice is not an end in itself: the budding pianist doesn't work her fingers on scales in order to play scales. She uses her fingers on scales to build muscle memory, so that her fingers can move the way they need to without her having to consciously think about it.

©Nick Stenning

The disciplines you use matter: merely thinking about the piano, listening to piano music, even building a piano will not make you a pianist. Building a piano won't train your fingers to manage arpeggios, but it will train your mind to understand the structure and operation of pianos.

Example – Patience

Let's say that you are impatient. You hop grocery lines, mentally competing against other shoppers to be in the fastest line. You curse the driver in front of you going at a lower speed than the one you want.

You do not become more patient by willing yourself to be patient. You become more patient by practicing thoughts and actions that in turn produce patience. Here are some disciplines that can help you train for patience:

» Picking the longest line in the grocery store every time.

» Driving at the speed limit in the slow lane, praying for the good of those who honk at you.

» Getting enough sleep.

» Meditation.

» Long distance running.

THE DIVINE CONSPIRACY

Introduction

Most explicitly framed in the book of the same name, the divine conspiracy is one of the foundational concepts for Dallas' theology. The conspiracy is the Trinity's methodology for establishing God's effective reign throughout God's creation, most especially in human hearts.

The divine conspiracy undermines the structures of evil with the forces of truth, freedom, and love. As part of the divine conspiracy humans are allowed to live an eternal kind of life in God's kingdom — under his reign — in our lives right now. It also calls for union with Jesus, accomplished through the renovation of his disciples' hearts and minds into Christ-likeness. And so Jesus' disciples "train to reign" alongside him, which simply means that through their effort and God's grace they should grow into free and powerful beings, worthy of God's trust and able to use his power wisely, who participate in the creation and rule over what is good.

The divine conspiracy is not a plan to get people forgiven and into heaven, but to get heaven into people so that they live an eternal kind of life, now and forever.

Definition

The divine conspiracy is God's plan to intervene in human history, overcoming evil with good, and creating "an all-inclusive community of loving persons, with Himself included in that community as its prime sustainer and most glorious inhabitant." (Dallas Willard, quoted in Richard Foster's *Celebration of Discipline*, page 189.)

Quotes

" ... his conspiracy to undermine the structures of evil, which continue to dominate human history, with the forces of truth, freedom and love." (DC 188)

"[In] the heart of the divine conspiracy, [humans reigning] just means to be free and powerful in the creation and governance of what is good." (DC 250)

Other relevant citations

DC 11: We are invited ... part of the divine conspiracy.

DC 30: Sometimes the places ... a crucial aspect of the conspiracy.

DC 384: God has made himself known ... how the divine conspiracy works ....

ETERNAL (KIND OF) LIFE

Introduction

"Now this is eternal life: that they know you, the only true God, and Jesus Christ, whom you have sent." (John 17:3, NIV) Knowledge, in Jesus' terms, is not simply awareness of some fact, but relationship with a person. Thus eternal life, better described as an eternal kind of life, is a life lived in interactive, cooperative, and communicative relationship with God in God's present and coming kingdom.

Though eternal life is never-ending, its main characteristic is not longevity but quality. It is a rich life, the fullness of which is experienced over time as a progression from "confidence in and reliance upon Jesus," leading to a "desire to be his apprentice" in living in and from the kingdom of God. The abundance of the life of apprenticeship then leads to *obedience*, and its associated disciplined life. In turn this leads to and is reinforced by the "*pervasive inner transformation of the heart and soul*" into Christ-likeness. That transformation provides the character it takes to be given "*power to work the works of the kingdom.*" (DC 366-68)

Definition

Eternal life is interactive covenant relationship among the Trinity with a human being. It is a life lived in interactive, cooperative, and communicative relationship with God in God's present and coming kingdom. The fullness of its dimensions is achieved over time through human effort and God's grace.

61

Quotes

"When we are like this, our whole life is an eternal one. Everything we do counts for eternity and is preserved there." (RH 41)

"Eternal life in the individual does not begin after death, but at the point where God touches the individual with redeeming grace and draws them into a life interactive with Himself and His kingdom. A new, non-human activity becomes a part of our life …. " (*Spiritual Formation as a Natural Part of Salvation*)

"[Actual] obedience to Christ as Lord would transform ordinary life entirely and bring those disciples who are walking with Christ together wherever their lives touch. Christians who are together in the natural stream of life would immediately identify with one another because of the radically different kind of life, the eternal kind of life, manifestly flowing in them." (GO 77)

Other relevant citations

GO xiv: The eternal life … apprenticeship to Jesus.

RH 25: [Christian assemblies should become schools for a] life that is eternal in quality now, as well as unending in quantity.

Example—Frank Laubach

Frank Laubach was a missionary acclaimed for developing the "Each One Teach One" literacy program. He was also a thoughtful recorder of his relationship with Christ, and his pursuit of a constant flow of awareness of God. His goal was to keep God before his mind at all times, to live all his waking moments listening to his inner voice—God's voice—as he imagined Jesus must have done.

He began by taking time each morning to settle himself into God's presence. As the day progressed, he brought God to mind on a regular basis, first sporadically, then every hour, then every minute.

He discovered that it was quite possible for him to hold two thoughts at once: that of whatever he was doing at the moment, and that of God's presence. This changed the quality of his life, as you can imagine, so that he felt himself carried along by God at all times.

Like Brother Lawrence before him, Laubach made clear that the life of the mystic is not mysterious, but a continual refocusing of your attention onto God. With effort and grace, it becomes second nature, and the eternal kind of life is at hand.

EVIL

Introduction

Dallas treated evil as neither an external entity (such as Satan) nor an inherent condition of the flesh. Instead, evil is activity of the mind and body that results in the destruction of what is good. Since evil is human activity, one cannot blame evil thought, intent, or action on someone else, or on the human condition, or any outside influence.

Evil is the outcome of one's understanding of "the good life" and how to achieve it: if what we believe *is* good is not in fact good, we will act evilly. If our beliefs make us the center of the universe, we will act to secure and enhance our place, resulting in our doing evil, mentally and physically. We are responsible for evil because we have the ability to control what we think and do.

The institutional evil we find in social systems is the result of the evil of human beings becoming the beliefs and habits of the system. To remove the evil within a system it is not enough to re-order the system. The evil of the people in the system—which is the result of a faulty understanding of what is good for humankind—must be addressed.

Definition

Evil is the intentional or habitual destruction or undermining of what is good in human life. It is lodged in bodily habits as well as the images and thoughts of the mind. Evil springs from self-idolatry or hubris—putting oneself in the position of god in place of God—and is overcome by restoring God and oneself to the proper places.

Quotes

1. Evil is the intentional or habitual destruction or undermining of what is good in human life.

"The person who is morally bad or evil is one who is intent upon the destruction of the various goods of human life with which they are effectively in contact, or who is indifferent to the existence and maintenance of those goods … This orientation of the will toward promotion of human goods is the fundamental moral distinction …"(*Moral Rights, Moral Responsibility and the Contemporary Failure of Moral Knowledge*)

2.   It is lodged in bodily habits as well as the images and thoughts of the mind.

"[In spiritual formation] the readinesses to do evil that inhabit our bodily members through long practice are gradually removed, to an ever-increasing degree." (GO 21)

"[Our] body must increasingly be poised to do what is good and refrain from what is evil. The inclinations to wrongdoing that literally inhabit its parts must be eliminated." (RH 159)

3.   Evil springs from self-idolatry or hubris—putting oneself in the position of god in place of God—and is overcome by restoring God and oneself to the proper places.

"[The] radical evil of the human heart [is] a heart that would make me God in place of God." (RH 54)

Other relevant citations

RH 99: Ideas and images … can even blind us to what lies plainly before us.

RH 106: [Worship] is the single most powerful … revealed truth confirmed in experience.

RH 170: This total yielding … no longer running the body and its parts.

SD 234: The monstrous evils we deplore … generally acceptable patterns of life.

66

FAITH

Introduction

Rather than being a wish, or a flaw in rational thinking, faith is a kind of knowledge. Like knowledge, faith is based on experience and reason, but faith is knowledge of the nonmaterial or spiritual realm.

Knowledge increases as one learns more about a topic, or becomes more deeply acquainted with a person, or spends more time and effort doing an activity. It is the same way with faith: one's faith increases with the evidence of information, companionship, or experience. What we call *blind* faith is really just entry-level faith, developed from abstract reasoning, or shallow acquaintance, or need and desire.

In the biblical tradition, faith has an element of confidence that can move one to action. For this reason, faith may also be called trust, since it conveys both knowledge and action based on that knowledge. The power of faith to influence or effect action is dependent on its breadth and depth. A superficial faith may impel you to move yourself; deep faith can enable you to move mountains.

Everyone has faith. The only question is what (or whom) one has faith *in*.

Definition

Faith is what knowledge is called when the knowledge is of something intangible or invisible. Faith has an element of confidence that moves one to action.

Quotes

1. Faith is what knowledge is called when the knowledge is of something intangible or invisible.

"Faith is not opposed to knowledge; it is opposed to sight." (HG 194)

"Most of what we think we see as the struggle *of* faith is really the struggle to act *as if* we had faith when in fact we do not." (HG 118)

2. Faith has an element of confidence that moves one to action.

"[Faith] is commitment to action, often beyond our natural abilities, based upon knowledge of God and God's ways." (KCT 20)

Other relevant citations

GO 110: [We] understand "saving faith" … what he did or said …

KCT 20: An act of faith in the biblical tradition … upon knowledge of God and God's ways.

KCT 156: And to come to [Jesus] in faith … his tutelage.

RH 129: Faith is confidence … "leap."

RH 129: [Faith] sees the reality … of God.

SD 41: [T]he New Testament knows nothing … social and political environment.

SD 65: The biblical worldview … tendency called "faith" …

SD 175: The cautious faith … not falling.

Example—Martin Luther on faith

Though we are concerned here with the nature of faith—what faith is—both Dallas and his Protestant forebears have focused on what faith does. Just as faith in a partner calms concern and enables happiness, so faith in God produces confidence and joy. Martin Luther explores this good-producing aspect of faith in his introduction to *Preface to the Letter of St. Paul to the Romans*:

"Faith is not that human illusion and dream that some people think it is…. Faith is a living, unshakeable confidence in God's grace; it is so certain, that someone would die a thousand times for it. This kind of trust in and knowledge of God's grace makes a person joyful, confident, and happy with regard to God and all creatures. This is what the Holy Spirit does by faith. Through faith, a person will do good to everyone without coercion, willingly and happily; he will serve everyone, suffer everything for the love and praise of God, who has shown him such grace."

© Glenn Fleishman

FALLEN(NESS)

Introduction

Our bodies are not the enemy. In fact, if we are "going on to perfection," to use John Wesley's phrase, we must engage the body in support of that effort. The body is an essential part of the human person. Even Adam and Eve had bodies—and even before they ate the apple!

Yet in many streams of Christian tradition there has been a sense that *fallenness*—as in the human condition after "the Fall" of Genesis 3—stains the very substance of bodies and things. In this view, Adam's disobedience, and God's response to it, corrupted every human being, perhaps every material object, from its origination. The corruption, the stain, the fallenness, is inherent in the materiality of the person or object. In extreme versions of this view, anything that is physical or tangible is bad.

Rather than focusing on the event of the Fall, Dallas directed his attention to humanity's state of fallenness. Fallenness is not an unchangeable attribute of physical things, but a painful contortion of the human soul in those who live without God.

Definition

Fallenness is the whole-person condition that comes about from mistrusting God, affecting all five basic aspects of the human person. Mistrusting God ruins, contorts, or breaks the human soul. It is expressed in the human body by its readiness to do evil, and in the social sphere by the results of the evil it does. Fallenness is evident in the human mind by self-dependence and egoism, and in the human will by its enslavement to desire. Fallenness expresses itself in the human spirit by an unrooted life, in which a person is alienated from God and therefore dependent upon his or her own energy and life force.

Quotes

1.   Fallenness is the whole-person condition that comes about from mistrusting God, affecting all five basic aspects of the human person. Mistrusting God ruins, contorts, or breaks the human soul.

"Not [the body with its powers] but its *deformed condition* is 'fallen human nature.' *In this condition* the flesh opposes the spirit, does that which is evil, and must be crucified to restrain it. ... Fallen human nature is a certain manner in which the good powers deposited at creation in our human flesh are twisted and organized against God. This comes about through processes that are social and historical as well as individual." (SD 90-91)

2.   Fallenness is not an unchangeable attribute of bodies, but their readiness to do evil.

"[The body] can acquire a 'life of its own'—tendencies to behave without regard to our conscious intentions. In our fallen world this life is prepossessed by evil, so that we do not have to think to do what is wrong, but must think and plan and practice—and receive grace—if we are to succeed in doing what is right. But Christ shows us how to bring the body from opposition to support of the new life he gives us, 'the Spirit' now in us." (GO 89)

3.   It is evident in the social sphere by the results of the evil human beings do.

"However we may picture the original event, "the fall," one cannot deny that such mistrust [of God] pervasively characterizes human life today and that things do not go well on earth." (DC 23)

4.   Fallenness is evident in the human mind by self-dependence and egoism, and in the human will by its enslavement to desire.

"The true effect of the Fall was to lead us to trust in the flesh alone, to 'not see fit to acknowledge God any longer' because we now suppose ... that, since there is no God to be counted on in the living of our lives, we must take things into our own hands ... It is the carnal

MIND—not the flesh—that is at enmity with God and incapable of subjection to his law." (SD 89-91)

5.   Fallenness expresses itself in the human spirit by an unrooted life, in which a person is alienated from God and therefore dependent upon his or her own energy and life force.

"In the biblical account of our fall from God, we were assigned to earn our bread by the sweat of our face. The sweat comes from our own energies, which is all we have left after losing our roots in God's own life." (DC 23)

Other relevant citations

RH 74: It is the controlling principle ... and other environment.

RH 102: Paul knew ... our ideas and images for his.

RH 204: When [the soul] is as it should be ... and nature at large.

SD 54: [The] death that befell ... in their experience.

SD 89-90: [W]e badly err in thinking of flesh ... now serves as primary host to sin.

SD 101: [Solitude is capable of breaking wills] because it excludes ... the sin-laden world.

SD 244-27: Above all, [our "why?" at evil] shows a failure ... it is very high in almost everyone.

Example—Structural integrity

Consider the design of a bridge. To perform adequately, without failure, the bridge needs everything to work as it should. The design, manufacture, and materials all must work properly and together; sabotage and destruction must not occur. If a bridge fails, something that did not have to go wrong, has.

Our old concept of fallenness suggests that there is something about bridges, that no matter how well they are made or out of what material, that makes them failures. In the olden days bridges used to be perfectly reliable and beautiful, but no longer, because what is now the nature of bridges undermines their reliability and beauty.

To torture the metaphor a bit more: the design of the bridge is like the human spirit; its materials like human body and mind; its manufacture like our soul; and the potential for sabotage like social interaction. For Dallas, there is nothing inherently bad about a bridge or a person; whatever causes failure can be remedied. People, like bridges, are meant to have structural integrity. The designer has done His job. It is up to the engineer, contractor, steelmakers, riveters, and all those who have power over the building of the bridge and its maintenance to ensure its integrity. If that is done, the bridge—and the person—will function as it should, without fail.

74

FELLOWSHIP

Introduction

In American churches, and maybe in others, *fellowship* has come to refer to those few minutes of idle chatter and bad coffee after Sunday services. In some, fellowship is the word used for the social program area of church life. Unfortunately, these uses may be perfectly appropriate, reflecting the shallowness of relationship found in church life.

In the Old Testament, fellowship is a kind of temple offering—a symbol and effecter of relationship between humanity and God. In the New Testament, the most common word translated as fellowship is *koinonia*, signifying the deep, invisible relationship between the people of the church. Fellowship is best thought of as a quality, rather than as an activity.

In line with the biblical use, Dallas uses the word *fellowship* in four related but distinguishable ways, referring to 1) a discipline; 2) a quality of love among Christians; 3) a mode by which God dwells in human beings and they relate to God; 4) and the gathering of Christians in the interactive presence of the Trinity.

Definition

Fellowship is a human relationship of transparency, honesty, righteousness, intimacy and depth: agape love; a reciprocal indwelling of God in a person and that person's joyful dependence upon God; a spiritual discipline; and the loving gathering of disciples together in the presence of the Trinity, enabling deep knowledge, sustaining them as individuals (and as a body), and making possible their constant glorification of God.
In short, fellowship is an agape quality of relationship, perfected in God's indwelling presence, and practiced among disciples as a spiritual discipline and as a gathering of love.

75

Quotes

1.   Fellowship is a human relationship of transparency, honesty, righteousness, intimacy and depth: agape love.

"In their relations to others, [the children of light] are completely transparent. Because they walk in goodness they have no use for darkness, and they achieve real contact or fellowship with others-especially other apprentices of Jesus." (RH 220)

2.   Fellowship is a reciprocal indwelling of God in a person and that person's joyful dependence upon God.

" ... the normal human life God intended for us: God's indwelling his people through personal presence and fellowship." (HG 18)

"[When] we bring the reflective will to life in Christ (birth "from above"), and add the instruction of the law and the presence of the Holy Spirit, along with the fellowship of his Body, we have the wherewithal to live in such a way that God is glorified in everything we do." (*Spiritual Formation and the Warfare Between the Flesh and the Spirit*)

3.   Fellowship is a spiritual discipline.

"What, though, makes confession bearable? Fellowship. There is an essential reciprocity between these two disciplines." (SD 189)

4.   Fellowship is the loving gathering of disciples together in the presence of the Trinity, enabling deep knowledge, sustaining them as individuals (and as a body), and making possible their constant glorification of God.

"[Valuable as it is, spiritual reading] cannot take the place of fellowship with other disciples living and walking beside us .... When we gather 'in the name' of Jesus, we gather to love one another and to be loved, to serve one another and be served ... So when we 'go to church,' we go to love those who are there and to be loved with his *agape* love .... It is of absolute importance that you get this right if you are to *know* Christ. We know Christ in others .... The most important thing about our fellowship with other disciples is that Jesus, the trinitarian presence, should be in our midst. For that, we must meet 'in his name'; that is, we meet for his purposes, with his resources, and in his presence." (KCT 157-59)

Other relevant quotes

GO 74: [Classic disciplines for life in the Spirit are] solitude and silence ... and the like.

RH 48: Most Christians have never ... knew to be right.

RH 132: For to the others ... community of love (John 13:34-35).

RH 136: Love, joy, and peace ... but increasingly less so.

SD ix: We can ... in the fellowship of his Father.

SD 186-87: In fellowship we engage ... Personalities united can contain more ... The Life is one that requires some regular and profound conjunction with others who share it.

SD 189: The highest level ... and restitution ...

Example—Bonhoeffer's Life Together

Dietrich Bonhoeffer's treatise on Christian community, Life Together, is perhaps the most well-known meditation on fellowship in the Christian canon. Inspired by his time developing Christian camaraderie in the underground seminary at Finkenwalde, along with its subsequent closure by the Nazis, Bonhoeffer wrote about the invisible church that stems from Christ and connects all Christians. This church—which is relationship wrought by Christ through the cross-is only available through him; it deepens and flourishes as its members increasingly turn their attention toward God and are sanctified by God.

"What determines our brotherhood is what that man is by reason of Christ. Our community with one another consists solely in what Christ has done to both of us. This is true not merely at the beginning, as though in the course of time something else were to be added to our community; it remains so for all the future and to all eternity. I have community with others and I shall continue to have it only through Jesus Christ. The more genuine and the deeper our community becomes, the more will everything else between us recede, the more clearly and purely will Jesus Christ and his work become the one and only thing that is vital between us. We have one another only through Christ, but through Christ we do have one another, wholly, for eternity." (Dietrich Bonhoeffer in *Life Together*, pages 25-26)

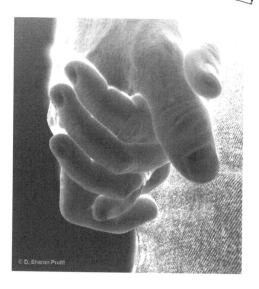

© D. Sharon Pruitt

Spiritual Formation

FIVE (OR SIX) ASPECTS OF THE HUMAN PERSON

Introduction

Some initial clarification may be helpful. The thorough reader of Dallas' work will notice that his enumeration of the aspects of the human person appears inconsistent. The fullest exposition, on pages 30-37 of *Renovation of the Heart*, delineates six: thought, feeling, choice, social context, body, and soul. However the diagram on page 38 names five, because thought and feeling are given the umbrella name *mind*. In the same diagram, *will* (or *spirit* or *heart*) replaces *choice*. Thereafter in *Renovation*, we usually (but not always) count five: mind, will/heart/spirit, social context, body, and soul. In chapter 7 of *The Great Omission*, he uses the list of six. In *The Divine Conspiracy* there is no list, but *mind* is the umbrella term for both thoughts and feelings.

Dallas also refers to these aspects in multiple ways: as aspects of *human life*, of the *self*, of the *person*, of the *personality*. He also uses *dimensions* in place of *aspects* from time to time.

All that said, Dallas used the five-aspect diagram very frequently in talks and classes, so five is what is discussed below. Please see the other entries in this dictionary for fuller discussion of each aspect.

Definition

The five aspects of the human person (*or* self *or* life *or* personality) are: mind (inclusive of both thoughts and feelings), body, will/heart/spirit (including choice), social context, and soul. Spiritual formation targets the first four, as transforming them heals the soul.

The diagram of the five aspects of the human person

"[In] this diagram the inner circles are not meant to exclude the outer ones, but to incorporate them in part: to be superimposed on them without exhausting them. But there is always more to what is represented by the outer circles than to what is represented by the inner.

Thus there is more to the mind than to the spirit (heart/will), though spirit intermingles with mind, and more to the body than to the mind, though mind intermingles with body, and so on. By making the soul the outer circle and interfacing it with an infinite environment, we indicate that it is the most inclusive dimension of the self, foundational to all others, but also that access to it may be achieved directly from sources entirely outside the person-from God, certainly, but possibly other forces as well, benign as well as dreadful.

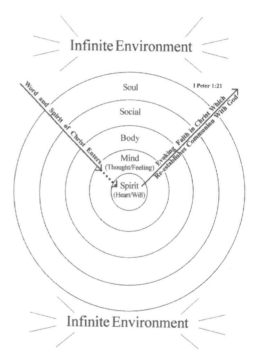

The outer wall of the soul is perhaps like a permeable membrane in a biological organism, which is designed to allow passage of some but not all foreign objects. When that wall is broken, individuals are at the mercy of forces they cannot handle. The soul can be sustained intact and can function as it is supposed to only in the keeping of God." (RH 38-39)

Other relevant citations

RH 30: Now, when we take a closer look ... Soul (the factor that integrates all of the above to form one life)

RH 32: The six "aspects," ... most inclusive object of redemption.

RH 39: Our actions ... the will alone.

RH 40-41: In the life away from God ... and the spirit, God.

Another explanation

On May 21, 2013, author and psychologist Bill Gaultiere responded beautifully to a question about the diagram of the five aspects posed to the Spiritual Formation Forum on the Dallas Willard Center's website.

"The spirit (heart or will) is in the middle because it's the center and it's designed to be the driver. We can chose to submit to God and his kingdom and rely on the Holy Spirit as we do what we're doing. To the extent that we do that our life becomes one of eternal living.

The soul is the largest, most encompassing part of the person. It's hard to understand because it's also the deepest part and integrates all the other components into one personality. It's meant to be in a flow of life. The Psalmist talks to his soul. The soul actually extends beyond our body and our social connections. When you're in a room with someone you pick up a 'vibe' from them.

The will, under God, is meant to be the source of our actions. The tricky part is that the will works off of our thoughts and feelings. Also we react (without thinking or making a conscious choice) to situations based on habits in our body. If you look close at the arrow pointing in you'll see dashed lines between mind and will. That's because these parts interact. So as the Word and Spirit come to us, at the first moment of salvation but also before and after, they may enter into the parts of our person, including our thoughts and affect our choices.

81

To be saved or belong to Christ means that the Holy Spirit has come to live in our hearts. Then we need to work on renewing our mind (thoughts and feelings), yielding our bodily members, connecting with other Christ-followers, and relying on God to restore our souls."

You can read more at http://dallaswillardcenter.com/forum/ best-practices-forum/question-needing-help-understanding/#p196.

FLESH

Introduction

Does this word bring to mind an illicit lowliness, a kind of inherent stain? There is good reason for that. In common use, flesh is the meat of an animal or the edible part of a fruit; both John's gospel and Paul's epistles tweak this meaning as they distinguish between flesh and spirit. John and Paul imported this distinction from the ancient Greeks, who had maintained hard divisions between material and spiritual, with the material being a poor imitation of the spiritual.

The flesh/spirit dichotomy hardened during the Middle Ages as the material, physical aspect of reality developed a sense of baseness: by the mid-15th century in England, the word *flesh* was heard as carnal, sensual, and most certainly not spiritual. But that particular overtone is not present in the New Testament, where *flesh* isn't necessarily carnal, or even strictly material. It is, however, subject to the influence of fallenness, especially in its habits, and its preparedness to do evil.

Why does all this matter? The Bible uses *flesh* and *fleshly* between one and three hundred times, depending on the translation, and not many of these uses imply sensuality or even strict physicality. Therefore it is important to distinguish between the meanings, and which one is meant where. So too in Dallas' work, as he uses the word 59 times in *Renovation of the Heart* alone!

[*Definition follows on next page.*]

Definition

Flesh is:

1. the *human body*—its "flesh and blood"—particularly as driven by desire, habit, and context;

2. the *powers and abilities* that are standardly—and somewhat independently from God—available to human beings as embodied creatures;

3. a description of *human impulse springing from desire*, more animal than spiritual;

4. a substance opposed to or distinguished from spirit; or

5. a metaphor for the *singular indivisible essence* of human beings. (*A rare usage*)

Briefly put, flesh is the material body of a human being, endowed with powers and abilities, and formed by context and desire. It acts out of habitual impulse, often independently of God according to its fallenness.

Flesh may also refer to the singular essence of human beings.

Quotes

1.   Flesh as the *human body*—its "flesh and blood"—particularly as driven by desire, habit, and context.

"The New Testament texts normally use the word "flesh" to refer to the human body formed in the ways of evil and against God ... shaped in a life context ... that is godless ... [and thus] are poised to sin." (GO 83)

2.   Flesh as the *powers and abilities* that are standardly—and somewhat independently from God—available to human beings as embodied creatures

"'Flesh' in its biblical usage seldom means the mere physical substance that makes up the parts of the body ... is generally spoken of in the Bible as something *active*, a specific power or range of powers

84

that is embedded in a body of a specific type, able or likely to do only certain kinds of things ... ." (SD 86)

3. Flesh (or fleshly) as a description of *human impulse springing from desire*, more animal than spiritual.

"In Galatians 5 Paul described 'the deeds of the flesh' when natural human impulses and abilities are allowed to be the rule of life." (RH 221)

4. Flesh as a substance opposed to or distinguished from spirit

"Thus in the final analysis it is true that 'flesh and blood cannot inherit the Kingdom of God.' But the flesh and blood *person* can inherit it. At the initiative and guidance of the spiritual word of God, a person's finite energies can be meshed with God's in such as way that progressively—and, eventually, totally—he or she can 'put on incorruption.'"(SD 88-89)

5. Flesh as a metaphor for the *singular indivisible essence* of human beings. (*A rare usage*)

"The intent in marriage is a union of two people that is even deeper than the union of parents and children or any other human relationship. They are to become 'one flesh,' one natural unit, building one life, which therefore could never lose or substitute for one member and remain a whole life." (DC 169)

Other relevant citations

DC 196: And our abundant strength ... are in secret.

GO 46: The flesh stands ... of human beings.

RH 65: To make my desires paramount ... a state of death.

RH 160: [The] "flesh" ... in the human body ...

RH 162: Incarnation is ... full redemption.

SD 90: Certainly it is true ... crucified to restrain it.

FORGIVENESS

Introduction

Somehow forgiveness became confused with approval. When you forgive a behavior that does not mean you approve of it. Forgiveness has also been confused with reconciliation, but the tearful meeting that mends broken relationship is not part of forgiveness. Forgiveness is much simpler than that. Forgiveness happens when you give up your right to revenge.

In God's case, forgiveness means that God forgoes the righteous vengeance that is God's alone. It is a necessary, grace-filled, yet insufficient piece of our relationship with God: as with any other relationship, our relationship with God does not thrive just because God has forgiven us. Thus the forgiveness that came at the cross of Christ is not the end of the story of our relationship with God. There is more to relationship than that.

In our relationships with others, thoroughgoing forgiveness is possible only through the awareness of God's mercy for us coupled with God's help in actually forgiving. It is impossible for us to be hardhearted if we accept and really know God's forgiveness.

In most works, Dallas writes of forgiveness in the context of God's mercy. However, he provides an extended discussion of forgiveness in chapter seven of *The Divine Conspiracy* as he addresses the Lord's Prayer.

Definition

Forgiveness is releasing another from any claims you might have to revenge or restitution.

Quotes

On God's forgiveness of us:

"We in one move find forgiveness for our sins and 'take his yoke upon us and learn of him' (Matthew 11:29, PAR). The idea that these can be separated is, as A. W. Tozer pointed out years ago, simply a modern heresy." (RH 242)

"Grace, you know, does not just have to do with forgiveness of sins alone." (GO 61)

On our forgiveness of others:

"We forgive someone of a wrong they have done us when we decide that we will not make them suffer for it in any way. This does *not* mean we must prevent suffering that may come to them as a result of the wrong they have done." (DC 262)

Other relevant citations

DC 262: We pray for help … cannot do it without help.

DC 263-64: Today we sometimes speak of people … I don't even understand it.

SD 33: Salvation is not … but a new order of life.

Example—Forgiving, forgetting, and forgoing abuse

One of the tragic misinterpretations of forgiveness is the idea that forgiving abuse requires reconciliation with or submission to one's abuser. The rationale goes something like this: if the abused person (child, wife, husband, employee) *really* loves like Jesus, then he or she will understand the pain of the abuser, forgive the actions that emerged from that pain, forget them and return to the relationship. This façade of forgiveness is sometimes shored up with verses about honoring your parents or submitting to your husband or slaves obeying their masters or forgiving your brother 70 x 7 times. In each case, the verse is being used to support the abuse, rather than to understand the nature of love.

To love is to "will the good" of another person. One can love—will the good—of an evil person without capitulating to the evil. Accepting this kind of love from God and practicing it with other people allows you to forgive—to give up your claims to revenge or restitution. But loving—willing the good—of another does not mean you allow that person to harm you. Nor does it require you to prevent the person's receiving the consequences of the behavior.

The restoration of relationship requires love, forgiveness, and change by all parties involved, for right relationship is reciprocal. But forgiving requires just one loving person, and the saving love of God.

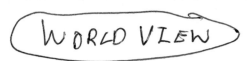
WORLD VIEW

THE FOUR GREAT QUESTIONS OF LIFE
(AND A FIFTH)

Introduction

The concept of ~~the four great questions~~ of life, also known as *the worldview questions* ~~is a pervasive~~ theme in Dallas' work. Formal discussion of the concept appears in both *Knowing Christ Today* and *The Great Omission*. Additionally, he frames two of the questions in chapter four of *The Divine Conspiracy*, articulating their answers through his analysis of the Beatitudes. These questions—and the answers to them—arguably provide the entire "why *this*" of Dallas' work.

Collectively, the four great questions aim to answer what counts as good for a human being, determining what counts as a good life. Each of us answers the questions for ourself, whether we realize it or not. Others can tell what our answers are by how we live our lives, as "a tree is recognized by its fruit." (Mt. 12:33, NIV) Dallas believed that all great teachers must teach answers to the four great questions; certainly Plato, the Buddha, and Freud all did that. The world answers them, of course, saying things like "the good life includes owning a BMW, being thin, and gaining fame for your work." Or, less conspicuously, one might think that the good life consists in unconstrained freedom and avoidance of pain.

As apprentices to Christ we may be led to ask, "Who are the people in my world who are pursuing the good life, but are deluded as to what it really is?" How we answer that in our own lives determines what kind of people we will be.

Dallas' mission was to answer the four great questions, to live the answers, and to bear their fruit.

The fifth question, posed in *Knowing Christ Today* and his lectures on theological epistemology, is this: how do we know which answers to the four questions are true?

Definition

The four great questions of life are:
What is real?
Who is well off?
Who is a genuinely good person?
How can I become a genuinely good person (and be well off)?

Quotes

"Jesus answers the four great questions of life: What is real? (God and His Kingdom.) Who is well off or 'blessed'? (Anyone alive in the Kingdom of God.) Who is a genuinely good person? (Anyone possessed and permeated with agape, God's kind of love.) And how can I become a genuinely good person? (By being a faithful apprentice of Jesus in Kingdom living, learning from him how to live my life as he would live my life if he were I.) …. These are the questions that every human being must answer, because of the very nature of life, and that every great teacher must address. Jesus Christ answers them in the gospels and, then, in his people in a way that becomes increasingly understandable and experimentally verifiable, and as no other person on earth has ever answered them." (GO 219)

"In the modern period in which we live, a fifth question has pushed its way to the forefront of human endeavor: How do we know which answers to the four questions are true? Its urgency for modern life and for contemporary issues is the result of the historical and — frankly — the political struggle between the traditional sources of guidance for life in the Western world, on the one hand, and sources derived from what may loosely be called 'science' or 'research,' on the other." (KCT 55-56)

Exercise—Jesus' answers, and yours

Dallas states that Jesus' answers to the Four Great Questions are 1) God and His Kingdom are real; 2) Anyone alive in the Kingdom is blessed; 3) A good person is one permeated with God's kind of love (agape); and 4) I can become a good person by being a faithful apprentice to Jesus on living in the Kingdom. Pretty compelling answers, right? But how would you, personally, recognize the real life examples of these answers? How would you know it when you saw it?

Discovering what counts for you as a concrete sign of "the good life" can help guide you on your way. We mentioned earlier that for some owning a BMW might be a sign they've achieved the good life. Spend some time in prayer, asking God to give you awareness of the goals or signs you use now to recognize the good life. You may not like what God shows you, so be ruthlessly non-judgmental as you write them down. Meditate on what you've written. Let the fact of it sink in. This may take time so don't rush. Then return to God, asking for goals or signs of the Kingdom good life. Write these down too. Meditate on them, letting them sink in. This will take even longer, as the gap between your signs and God's signs become apparent.

When you're ready, consider some disciplines—tactics for indirectly effecting changes in habit or character—you could use to move from believing one list to believing the other. Then begin. When you change the way you think and what you believe, God will help you change your character to match.

FREEDOM

Introduction

In modern North America when we speak of freedom we are usually talking about one of two things. One kind is the ability to take an action legally, such as owning a handgun, turning right on a red light, or getting married. The other is the absence of physical restraints, such as shackles, or social restraints, such as disapproval. This kind of freedom is *external,* allowing particular actions to be taken without fear of someone else's response.

External freedom was not Dallas' spiritual concern. When he wrote of freedom, he was speaking to a person's internal ability to choose and create without constraint. Internal constraints include things like habits of mind or body, addictions, viewpoints, and sin. A truly free person is able to choose and create without being bound by internal constraints such as these. A free person is largely self-determining: able to choose where to direct her attention, what to allow into her mind, and how to use her thoughts and body.

Though a free person may not be completely relieved of these constraints, she may be free from their ultimate influence. So while sin may be part of the context of a free person's choices, it will not be the deciding factor. While habit may influence her activities, it will not be the ultimate controller. The greatest freedom is the power to consistently choose the good when evil is an option.

Definition

Freedom is the ability to choose and create without internal constraint, particularly sin. Ultimately freedom is the power to consistently choose against evil. It is to consistently want the good and be able to do it. This power is developed through the availability of the new life in Christ and the retraining of the body and mind through discipline.

Quotes

1. Freedom is the ability to choose and create without internal constraint, particularly sin.

"[The] center point of the spiritual in humans as well as in God is self-determination, also called freedom and creativity." (DC 81)

2. Freedom is the power to consistently choose against evil. It is to consistently want the good and be able to do it.

"They will want the good and be able to do it, the only true human freedom." (RH 65)

3. Freedom is developed through the availability of the new life in Christ and the retraining of the body and mind through discipline.

"The primary freedom we have is always the choice of where we will place our minds." (GO 155)

"[W]e cannot always reliably and inexhaustibly submit our members to righteousness directly in performance ... In the hurly-burly of daily life I may not be able to speak the truth always. But, as a discipline, I can perhaps make myself return to those to whom I have lied ... marvelously enhanc[ing] my ability to speak the truth on other occasions .... Whatever activity of this type may be required to free me up, I must undertake it ... And if I do not submit my actions through the disciplines that fit my personality, I will not enter into the powerful, virtuous new life in a psychologically real way." (SD 120)

Other relevant citations

RH 33: Volition, or choice ... is power to do what is good—or evil.

SD 92-93: The very substance of our bodies ... the meaning of our freedom and of our responsibility.

SD 115: To be dead to sin ... Doing what is good and right becomes increasingly easy, sweet, and sensible to us as grace grows in us.

Example – Freedom in chains

Let's be clear: it is never good to be enslaved or imprisoned. These are not conditions of the good life. Yet we have all heard of people who suffered external constraint and internal freedom. Jesus, of course, appearing before Pilate and hanging on the cross, was free to think of God and love his accusers. Paul and Silas were trapped in prison, yet loudly sang God's praises. Felicita and Perpetua were arrested as catachumens, imprisoned, and martyred, yet remained faithful. More recently, we have before us Martin Luther King, Jr., Nelson Mandela, Dietrich Bonhoeffer, Esther Anh Kim, and many others. External freedom relies on the whims and battles of others. Internal freedom relies on self-mastery and God-submission.

© Christine Chua

GLORY

Introduction

Dallas didn't much use *glory* as a technical term, requiring special definition. Most commonly when he used the word he was quoting Bible passages such as Colossians 1:27 (... the glorious riches of this mystery, which is Christ in you, the hope of glory). But the picture of glory Dallas paints goes so far beyond the typical "bright light of heaven" idea that it merits some comment here. God's glory glows. It is of the same substance as energy. It is the marvelous relationship among the members of the Trinity. Glory *is* the image of God, and it is reflected utterly in creation as a whole and in the face of Jesus in particular. Your view of glory is what you are able to apprehend of the present fire of the presence of God.

Definition

Glory is the magnificent outpouring of the radiant splendor of God's power, strength, beauty, and goodness. Glory constantly fills the universe, permeating all of God's creation, and substantiating the kingdom of heaven. It is fully reflected in the person of Jesus, and is accessible to our participation in it through adoration of Jesus and obedience to him.

Quotes

1.   Glory is the magnificent outpouring of the radiant splendor of God's power, strength, beauty, and goodness.

"The glory of God, which is the effulgence of strength, power, and goodness, permeates the world and our lives now, but is hidden. Since we can enjoy some measure of eternal living now, we may shine with God's glory now." (*Personal notes from the Renovaré Institute, March 2011*)

2.   Glory constantly fills the universe, permeating all of God's creation, and substantiating the kingdom of heaven.

"I must learn to enjoy what I have created. God does not resent our liking what we've done. There is a glory to matter. Our activity of creation is seeing the creation of God and working with it— everything created is designed to praise God and reflect his glory. There is glory hidden in every bit of his creation." (*Personal notes from the Renovaré Institute, March 2011*)

"God glows. God's riches in glory—-that's talking about inexhaustible energy of personality, not just matter." (*Personal notes from the Renovaré Institute, March 2011*)

"What was the glory Jesus had with the Father before the world? It was this marvelous complement of these persons sharing life together: "That they may all be one; even as You, Father, are in Me and I in You, that they also may be in Us, so that the world may believe that You sent Me. The glory which You have given Me I have given to them, that they may be one, just as We are one; I in them and You in Me, that they may be perfected in unity, so that the world may know that You sent Me, and loved them, even as You have loved Me." (*Personal notes from the Renovaré Institute, March 2011*)

3.   It is fully reflected in the person of Jesus, and is accessible to our participation in it through adoration of Jesus and obedience to him.

"Our minds and values have to be restructured before God's glory …." (HG 112)

"Salvation is … participating in the life that Jesus is now living. Christ in me, the hope of Glory. That was the message to the Gentiles, as reported in Colossians, and that's the message to everyone. The 'Hope of Glory' is the living Christ in you and that's another way of describing life in the Kingdom of God." (*The Gospel of the Kingdom*)

"The key, then, to loving God is to see Jesus, to hold him before the mind with as much fullness and clarity as possible. It is to adore him…. First, we see his beauty, truth, and power while he lived among us as one human being among others…. The radiant person of Jesus shines forth from them up to the present day." (*Living a Transformed Life Adequate to Our Calling*)

100

Other relevant citations

GO 28: What brings about our transformation ... for this comes from the Lord, the Spirit.

GO 77: The lamp that is aglow ... by direct efforts at union.

Exercise—Haloes in heaven

For centuries, painters and other artists have inscribed perfect little circles of light around the head of Jesus. These golden circles appear with saints too, and angels. In the iconography and symbolisms of art, haloes represent holiness.

Artists also use a more translucent, diffuse light to symbolize God's presence. In art, God is in the light. Better said: God's glory imposes the light. That softly filtered gleam is a miniscule glimpse into the glory that is God and surrounds God. We are afforded the tiniest luminescence, the sweetest taste of the overpowering presence of God. The haloes of angels and saints are but the dust of glory that has fallen from God upon those near him.

Here is a question for meditation: assuming angels and saints and Jesus have haloes of some sort, whether circles or ephemeral wisps, could you see them in heaven? Would not their glory fade into the far greater effulgence, the utter and complete presence of God?

No wonder we do not always recognize the children of light among us: the halo of the earthbound saint is likewise swallowed up into the magnificence of Light.

GOD'S INTENT FOR US

Introduction

Getting into heaven isn't the point. God isn't merely trying to redeem us from an eternity of hellfire and brimstone, or to get us to being nice to each other now. God's intent for humanity is much grander: to become full persons who can reign with him. To do this we must come to resemble as much as possible the one human being suited to reigning alongside God, that is, Jesus. In this life, Jesus' disciples are in fact training to reign.

God is a sovereign committed to power-sharing arrangements. Our task is to become trustworthy.

> ## Definition
>
> God's intent for us is to become Christ-like persons who can live in God's presence with the power to do what we want as, lovingly and creatively, we reign alongside and in union with him over his kingdom for eternity.

Quotes

1. God's intent for us is to become Christ-like persons …

"We can be very sure that this is God's intent for us … to be 'rooted and grounded in love' and 'know the love of Christ which surpasses knowledge, that you may be filled up to all the fullness of God' (Ephesians 3: 17-19)." (RH 137-38)

2. … who can live in God's presence.

"The aim of God in history is to create an all-inclusive community of loving persons with Himself included in that community as its prime sustainer and most glorious inhabitant." (Dallas Willard, quoted by Richard Foster in *Celebration of Discipline*, page 189)

"God's intent is to be present among his people and to heal them, teach them, and provide for them." (RH 246)

3.   ... with the power to do what we want

"You see, God has very high aims for you and me. His aim is that each one of us becomes the kind of person he can empower to do what we want .... Now you recognize that a lot of work has to be done on our "wanter" before that can happen. But that is what life is about." *(Knowing How to Acknowledge God)*

4.   ... as, lovingly and creatively, we reign alongside and in union with him over his kingdom for eternity.

"[We] learn step by step how to govern, to reign with him in his kingdom. To enter and to learn this reign is what gives the individual life its intended significance." (DC 250)

Other relevant citations

DC 22: God equipped us ... his love for us means in practical terms.

DC 369: Yet it is God's intent ... to his great joy and relief, no doubt.

KCT 160: Prayer is God's arrangement ... to bless the world through us.

SD 48: People were ... this rule to which we are appointed.

SD 54: [S]o long as men and women ... Creator of all things.

Spiritual Formation

THE GOLDEN TRIANGLE OF SPIRITUAL GROWTH

Introduction

Dallas insisted that churches that intended to help people develop Christlike character needed a curriculum for Christlikeness. In *The Divine Conspiracy* he provided a loose model for such a curriculum. Dallas called the visual image of the model *the golden triangle of spiritual growth*, though in *The Great Omission* he named it *the golden triangle of spiritual formation*. Whether the triangle represents the process of growth or formation, Dallas used the golden triangle extensively in his lectures and classes. The following is a reconstruction of his model.

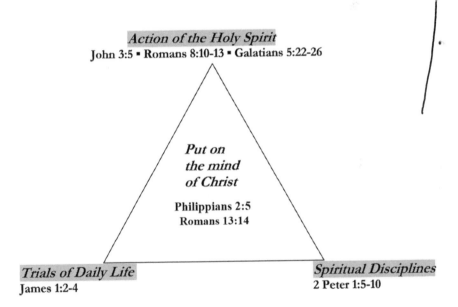

Action of the Holy Spirit
John 3:5 • Romans 8:10-13 • Galatians 5:22-26

Put on the mind of Christ

Philippians 2:5
Romans 13:14

Trials of Daily Life
James 1:2-4

Spiritual Disciplines
2 Peter 1:5-10

Definition

The golden triangle of spiritual formation (or growth) represents a model of the curriculum for Christlikeness. The point of such a curriculum is the transformation of the whole person through the restoration of the spirit, the renewal of the mind, and the habits of the body.

Explanation

One point (or side) of the triangle is your daily life, particularly the trials and challenges that test your mettle. Your daily life is the proving ground for character traits such as perseverance, patience, acceptance, and joy. With these, you can discover the power and wholeness of God's kingdom rule.

"Consider it pure joy, my brothers and sisters, whenever you face trials of many kinds, because you know that the testing of your faith produces perseverance. Let perseverance finish its work so that you may be mature and complete, not lacking anything" (James 1:2-4 NIV).

One point (or side) of the triangle is deliberate awareness of and interaction with God's lifegiving Spirit. God's Spirit, active in your life, is who provides the strength and guidance needed to pass through life's trials. Through the Spirit, the aspects of a Christlike character are developed.

"So I say, walk by the Spirit, and you will not gratify the desires of the flesh...the fruit of the Spirit is love, joy, peace, forbearance, kindness, goodness, faithfulness, gentleness and self-control. Against such things there is no law... Since we live by the Spirit, let us keep in step with the Spirit." (Galatians 5:16, 22-23, 25, NIV)

One point (or side) of the triangle are the disciplines for the spiritual life. Spiritual disciplines use the mind to engage the body. Through these efforts of your body you break the habits of the flesh

106

that render you ready to act badly, and develop those habits of body and mind that enable you to act freely with God.

"For this very reason, make every effort to add to your faith goodness; and to goodness, knowledge; and to knowledge, self-control; and to self-control, perseverance; and to perseverance, godliness; and to godliness, mutual affection; and to mutual affection, love. For if you possess these qualities in increasing measure, they will keep you from being ineffective and unproductive in your knowledge of our Lord Jesus Christ. But whoever does not have them is nearsighted and blind, forgetting that they have been cleansed from their past sins …. Therefore, my brothers and sisters, make every effort to confirm your calling and election. For if you do these things, you will never stumble …" (2 Peter 1:5-10, NIV)

Inside the triangle is the overall context: the renewal of your mind through interactive knowledge of God so that you may put on the mind of Christ.

"Therefore if you have any encouragement from being united with Christ, if any comfort from his love, if any common sharing in the Spirit, if any tenderness and compassion, then make my joy complete by being like-minded, having the same love, being one in spirit and of one mind …. In your relationships with one another, have the same mindset as Christ Jesus …" (Philippians 2:1-2, 5, NIV)

THE GOOD LIFE

Introduction

There used to be a bumper sticker that read, "Whoever dies with the most toys wins." That was someone's view of having a good life. Every human being seeks the good life. All concepts of the good life have one thing in common: the good life serves one's interests when one lives it, providing overall well-being. The only differences among us are how we define the good life, what counts as well-being, and what means we use to achieve it.

The good life is the subject of what Dallas called *the four great questions* that every teacher of living must answer. In *The Divine Conspiracy* Dallas frames those four questions as two sets; together these two sets are intended to help us define the good life and the means to achieving it. The first set asks about the qualities of the good life itself: "Which vision of the good life is right? That is, what is genuinely in my interest, and how do I enter true well-being?" The second set asks about the qualities of the person who enjoys the good life: "Who is truly a good person, and how do I become one?"

Definition

The good life is the one that genuinely serves the interest of the person living it, and through which he finds well-being. For Jesus and his disciples this is a life lived in the reality of God's present kingdom. The good person is one who is living the good life, and whose inner life is as it should be: pervaded with love.

Quotes

"Jesus answers the four great questions of life: What is real? (God and His Kingdom.) Who is well off or 'blessed'? (Anyone alive in the Kingdom of God.) Who is a genuinely good person? (Anyone possessed and permeated with agape, God's kind of love.) And how can I become a genuinely good person? (By being a faithful apprentice of Jesus in Kingdom living, learning from him how to live my life as he would live my life if he were I.)" (GO 219)

"The morally good person is a person who is devoted to advancing the various goods of human life with which they are effectively in contact, in a manner that respects their relative degrees of importance and the extent to which the actions of the person in question can actually promote the existence and maintenance of those goods. Thus, moral goodness is a matter of the organization of the human will called 'character.'" (*Why It Matters If You Are Moral*)

"The morally good person is, I suggest, to be thought of as one who is admired and imitated just for what he or she is, and without any essential reference to specific relationships, talents, skills or useful traits they may have." (*Faith, Hope and Love as Indispensible Foundations of Moral Realization*)

Other relevant citations

DC 130: Having illustrated concretely…Jesus then proceeds…

SD ix: Here I want to deal with … the heart of the New Testament message.

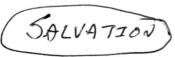

THE GOSPEL OF ATONEMENT

Introduction

Generally speaking, atonement theories of salvation suggest that Jesus was crucified to make up for the sins of the rest of us. In the last few centuries, and particularly in modern evangelicalism, profession of Jesus' atonement for our sins has been the defining act of Christian identity, the act that brings salvation. Dallas referred to this -- making profession of the particular theology both necessary and sufficient for salvation—as the *gospel of the atonement*. In the gospel of the atonement, getting into heaven is enough, and that is gained by believing a particular theology.

He argued that this overemphasis has created a division between salvation and discipleship that Jesus never intended. The result is that people believe they can be Christians without ever becoming disciples: if they believe that Jesus did X, no further action is needed because no greater outcomes can be achieved.

Dallas did not discuss atonement theories in his books or articles. He did not opine whether Jesus' death was a sacrifice, or a punishment, or a ransom. This silence should not be interpreted as a rejection of atonement, but an argument for a fuller understanding of the gospel message. His work is about how the disciple should live, rather than why it is Jesus "had to" die.

Definition

The gospel of atonement is the idea that Jesus' death on the cross made up for the sins of humankind, allowing or purchasing God's forgiveness, and that this is the bulk of salvation.

Quotes

"What has basically happened is that the meaning of 'Trust Christ' has changed. It has come to no longer mean trusting Him; it meant trust something He did. In that way, one theory of the atonement was substituted for the Christian Gospel. The results of this are that (now) discipleship is not essential, and people are not invited to become disciples." (*Subversive Interview - Part 1*)

"What you present as the gospel will determine what you present as discipleship. If you present as the gospel what is essentially a theory of the atonement and you say if you accept this theory of the atonement, your sins are forgiven and when you die you will be received into heaven, there is no basis for discipleship .... But if your gospel focuses on the gospel of the kingdom, that we are invited to live in the kingdom of God then the basis for discipleship becomes clear. The new birth should be seen as an entrance into the kingdom of God. John chapter 3 is not a 'forgiveness of sins' passage but a new life from above passage. Forgiveness from sins is essential—but it is not the whole package." (*Kingdom Living*)

THE GOSPEL OF THE KINGDOM (OR THE GOSPEL OF JESUS)

(handwritten: Kingdom of God)

Introduction

What is the gospel message? In recent decades, the popular meaning of Jesus' birth, life, death, and teaching has been pared down to two mutually exclusive shreds. The first is that Jesus came to save you from the punishment for sin in the fires of hell, which he accomplished by his death. The second is that Jesus came to teach you how to end human evil and bring about heaven on earth through the overhaul of social systems. What they have in common is a single-minded focus on human evil and sin and what Jesus has done about them. Dallas calls this focus *the gospel of sin management.*

In contrast, he presents the *gospel of Jesus* (or *gospel of the kingdom*). This is the idea that Jesus' purpose is to proclaim the current availability of life in the kingdom of God. Life in the kingdom of God is not an after-death experience only, and it is not brought about by humans focused on solving social ills. Life in the kingdom of God is brought about by an individual having confidence in the truth that Jesus is all he says he is, following his way, and living an interactive, power-filled, intimate life with God now. This gospel is taught throughout the New Testament, but fleshed out in Matthew 5 through 7.

In emphasizing the gospel of the kingdom Dallas was not denying that justification came through Christ's death of the cross. He was expanding beyond the overly simplistic concern about getting into heaven, and suggesting there is more to salvation than justification. Neither was he suggesting that the improvement of life for the poor and the oppressed doesn't matter, or that wrongs shouldn't be righted. He was stating that changing the systems doesn't change the people, but transformed people cannot help but effect change by their very presence in the world.

Quotes

1. While the current content of the gospel is sin management—salvation from the consequences of sin …

"History has brought us to the point where the Christian message is thought to be essentially concerned only with how to deal with sin: with wrongdoing or wrong-being and its effects … . When we examine a broad spectrum of Christian proclamation and practice, we see that the only thing made essential on the right wing of theology is forgiveness of the individual's sins. On the left it is removal of social or structural evils. The current gospel then becomes a "gospel of sin management." Transformation of life and character is *no* part of the redemptive message. Moment-to-moment human reality in its depths is not the arena of faith and eternal living." (DC 41)

2. Life in the kingdom of God is accessible now, in this life …

"The faith by which Jesus Christ lived, his faith in God and his kingdom, is expressed in the gospel that he preached. That gospel is the good news that the kingdom rule of God is available to humankind here and now." (HG 156)

"Eternal life in the individual does not begin after death, but at the point where God touches the individual with redeeming grace and draws them into a life interactive with Himself and His kingdom. A new, non-human activity becomes a part of our life …." (*Spiritual Formation as a Natural Part of Salvation*)

3. … to all who trust Jesus and follow him in his way of living daily life.

"[The] gospel of the entire New Testament is that you can have new life now in the Kingdom of God if you will trust Jesus Christ. Not just something he did, or something he said, but trust the whole person of Christ in everything he touches—which is everything." (GO 61)

Other relevant citations

DC 49: In the Gospels ... Jesus the Anointed.

DC 122: The gospel of the kingdom ... everyone.

DC 222: [T]he gospel of the kingdom ... and to know it.

DC 273-74: His gospel is a gospel *for life and* .... apprentice in kingdom living.

RH 67: [Jesus] came proclaiming access ... is now available to you" ...

THE GOSPELS ~~ON THE LEFT AND~~ ON THE RIGHT (*AND* THE GOSPEL OF SIN MANAGEMENT)

Introduction

The terms *gospel on the left* and *gospel on the right* refer to the thin formulations of theology associated with liberal Christians and conservative Christians respectively. Both formulations have a theology of salvation, a theology of the Kingdom of God, a theology of formation, a theology of the identity of Jesus, and so forth. Both formulations can lead to a form of Christianity that neither requires nor trains for personal righteousness or social responsibility. Neither promotes a concept of real transformation of substance, soul, or character, nor do they tend to produce apprentices to Jesus. Both tend to produce Christians who mentally assent to some proposition *about* God, but who are not in interactive relationship *with* God. These non-disciple Christians have faith in things *about* Jesus, but do not *know* him, nor God through him.

We might call the gospel on the left the *social gospel* and the gospel on the right the *atonement gospel*.

The social gospel is that the good news that Jesus brought was of a society in which wrongs would be righted, wealth would be equitable, and everyone would just get along. This is the Kingdom of God. Jesus was one of the great teachers, if not the greatest. He was perhaps divine, perhaps not, but his example of goodness is the point. In the gospel on the left God tends to be seen as distant and mysterious, a watchmaker who set time and world in order and left it for humans to mess up or maintain.

The atonement gospel is the good news that Jesus, the son of God, was born to die. He died to atone for the sins of humankind, and for yours personally. That is, God has a right to exact punishment from us for the wrongs we have done, and Jesus took upon himself the deaths of humankind to satisfy God and spare us. Accept that this idea

117

is true and you will be saved from hell after you die, the rightful punishment for sin, in order to go to heaven, which is the Kingdom of God.

In Dallas' construction, the gospels of the right and the left come down to the same thing—a gospel of sin management—rather than a gospel of the kingdom.

Quotes

"Now on the Liberal side, they don't talk about sin or heaven when you die, they don't even talk about that. They talk about getting involved in social issues and then if you're really serious you'll join Sojourners and help out in the soup lines and protesting the war, and all sorts of things like that. But they're not going to put their lives on the line for that. They have a mild little version of what they would call discipleship which is about being engaged, or at least concerned about, social issues." (*Gospel of the Kingdom*)

"All notable theological and ecclesiastical positions with which I am familiar in the contemporary world hold that you can be right with God in ways that do not require transformation and in ways that do not routinely support and advance transformation. These ways may involve (1) professing right doctrine, (2) a specified form association with a denomination or group, or—on the more liberal side—(3) a kind of vague—or even intense— sympathy with what one takes Jesus to stand for. ... Now within this broad range of Christians, a narrower group—many Roman Catholics, Orthodox, and Evangelicals—think of "salvation" or "being saved" as strictly a matter of having one's sins forgiven and of having heaven "nailed down" as a result. ... what is essential, no matter the words, is receiving forgiveness by counting on the merits of Christ to cover your sin-debts." (*Spiritual Formation as a Natural Part of Salvation*)

Other relevant citations

DC 41: When we examine a broad spectrum ... is not the arena of faith and eternal living.

118

Example—The legality of abortion

To see the gospel of sin management at work, you need look only at some common disagreement among Christians, such as whether abortion should ever be legal. One line of rhetoric of conservative Christianity states that since abortion is a moral wrong, it should not be legal. One argument of liberal Christianity is that since abortions will happen, it is best that they are safe and legal. These particular arguments focus on limiting the frequency of the activity, that is, controlling the sin.

Another conservative argument is that abortion is a symbol and signal of moral decay; the way to avoid abortions is to attack the sources of moral decay and teach purity. A parallel liberal argument states that abortion is a symbol and signal of damaged social structures, such as poverty and lack of medical resources; the way to avoid abortions is to provide fiscal, education, and medical resources. These particular arguments aim at determining the root cause and circumstances of the choice to have an abortion.

In both cases, the pivot points are the activity of abortion and its moral or social impetus: the sin and its causes. A different take on the disagreement might note that people who are walking in relationship with Christ and being transformed by his grace and their effort into Christlikeness are likely to make different choices than those who are not, whether they are women and men engaged in sexual relationship, or the families and communities that surround them with support or condemnation. In this case, the focus is on the character of Christ followers and the actions that flow from that character.

GRACE

Introduction

The full history of the theology of grace influenced Dallas' use of the term. Frequently he mentioned Wesleyan *means of grace* as a way of understanding activities of faith, such as spiritual disciplines or liturgical elements. But while other theologies of grace make it seem like a blessing as permeating as air, or an instrument as precisely aimed as a missile, Dallas viewed grace more like fuel: a power from God that feeds an activity, enabling other good things to happen. Thus grace is neither a life preserver thrown to a recovering sinner, nor an anointing of one's good efforts. Grace is the power that fuels the extra-ordinary work of saints, and enables the rest of us to achieve greater things.

Definition

Grace is the power that fuels the extra-ordinary work of saints, and enables the rest of us to achieve greater things. While grace cannot be earned or deserved, through methodical effort we can enhance our ability to utilize and experience grace. Since grace is an active power of God's, the more we rely on God's power rather than our own, the more of God's grace we will consume. God's grace is what enables adherence to the law, release from the power of sin, death to self, and rest in the hands of God.

Quotes

1. Grace is the power that fuels the extra-ordinary work of saints, and enables the rest of us to achieve greater things.

   "Grace is God acting in our lives to accomplish what we cannot do on our own." (KCT 159)

2. While grace cannot be earned or deserved, through methodical effort we can enhance our ability to utilize and experience grace.

121

"Grace is not opposed to effort, it is opposed to earning. Earning is an attitude. Effort is an action. Grace, you know, does not just have to do with forgiveness of sins alone." (GO 61)

3.   Since grace is an active power of God's, the more we rely on God's power rather than our own, the more of God's grace we will consume.

"The true saint burns grace like a 747 burns fuel on takeoff. Become the kind of person who routinely does what Jesus did and said. You will consume much more grace by leading a holy life than you will by sinning, because every holy act you do will have to be upheld by the grace of God. And that upholding is totally the unmerited favor of God in action." (GO 162)

"To 'grow in grace' means to utilize more and more grace to live by, until everything we do is assisted by grace. Then, whatever we do in word or deed will all be done in the name of the Lord Jesus … " (RH 93)

4.   God's grace is what enables adherence to the law, release from the power of sin, death to self, and rest in the hands of God.

"The presence of the Spirit and of grace is not meant to set the law aside, but to enable conformity to it from an inwardly transformed personality." (RH 214)

Other relevant citations

SD 4-5: We are saved by grace … in the moment of need.

RH 25: Grace does not rule … grace.

RH 40: By standing in the correct relation … reorder the soul.

RH 42: What was then true … we have never been before.

RH 71: At the first we must very self-consciously … our occasions of self-denial.

RH 82: [We] consume the most grace … unintelligible.

RH 93: The greatest saints … like breath.

RH 164: Because we are in the grip … as we allow it.

RH 214: The presence of the Spirit … in terms of actions.

Example—Pull the wagon

The Mississippi Mass Choir had a song called "Pull the Wagon" in which a young boy is caught doing wrong by his even younger sister, who then extorts him into pulling her around all summer in her little red wagon in order to gain her silence. Eventually the summer's guilt and hard work wear the little boy down. He confesses his error to his mother, who had witnessed both the wrong and her son pulling his sister all over creation in the hot Mississippi sun. Of course she

forgives him. His shame and guilt are relieved, as is his suffering. At the end of the song, the little boy informs his sister he isn't pulling the wagon anymore.

The mother's silent witness and easy forgiveness represent God's grace. It is a compassion familiar to Christians, who recognize themselves in the sinning child afraid to face the consequences. But there is more to grace than the moment of mercy that rescues us from ourselves. Grace is not merely compassion, or mercy, or love. Grace is not just the inescapable goodness of God that washes all of creation. Grace is an active power of God, working in and through us, that enables a person to do otherwise impossible things. The activity of grace is what makes it possible for the boy to go to his mother in the first place, and what will help him do the right thing sooner the next time.

As adults, we can pull the wagon a very long time before we decide to go to our mothers, if we ever do. True acceptance of God's power and care takes practice, and need alone won't make us do it.

123

But we can learn to accept grace more fully and easily as we thoughtfully and repeatedly surrender our self-dependence and pride.

GREAT COMMISSION

THE GREAT OMISSION

Introduction

In 1910 G.K. Chesterton wrote, "The Christian ideal has not been tried and found wanting. It has been found difficult; and left untried" (*What's Wrong with the World*, Cassell & Company, Ltd., London 1910). A hundred years later the idea is not that living a different sort of life is difficult, but that it is utterly unnecessary. To be a "Christian", at least in mainstream evangelical theology, often requires only that one profess a particular version of atonement theology. Living a Christian ideal—or even living thoughtfully—is seen as an added dimension to Christian faith. Discipleship is what fanatics or heretics do.

Though Dallas' use of the term great omission came later, the concept underlies all of Dallas' books. The idea is simple: very few people who call themselves Christian actually do anything differently than do non-Christians, and churches have no systematic plan for changing that. So when we read Matthew 28:19-20, "Go and make disciples of all nations, baptizing them in the name of the Father and of the Son and of the Holy Spirit, and teaching them to obey everything I have commanded you," we skip over the "making" part and the "teaching" part, and settle for the "baptizing" part. That skipping over is the great omission.

Definition

The *great omission* is that we can be Christians without being disciples. That is, we have the false idea that we can believe certain ideas about Jesus without trusting him enough to learn from him how to live every moment of our lives.

Quotes

1.   The *great omission* is that we can be Christians without being disciples.

"What I call 'the great omission from the great commission' is the fact that Christians generally don't have a plan for teaching people [to] do everything that he commanded. We don't as a rule even have a plan for learning this ourselves, and perhaps assume it is simply impossible. And that explains the yawning abyss today between being Christian and being a disciple. We have a form of religion that has accepted non-obedience to Christ, and the hunger for spirituality and spiritual formation in our day is a direct consequence of that."
(*Spiritual Formation: What It Is and How It Is Done*)

2.   We have the false idea that we can believe certain ideas about Jesus without trusting him enough to learn from him how to live every moment of our lives.

"[A] biblical Christian is not just someone who holds certain beliefs *about* the Bible. He or she is also someone who *leads the kind of life demonstrated* in the Bible: a life of personal, intelligent interaction with God. Anything less than this makes a mockery of the priesthood of the believer." (HG 103-04)

"Our confidence in him is not merely a matter of believing things about him, however true and important they may be. Indeed, no one can actually believe the truth about him without trusting him by intending to obey him. It is a mental impossibility. To think otherwise is to indulge a widespread illusion that now smothers spiritual formation in Christlikeness among professing Christians and prevents Christian spiritual formation from naturally spreading worldwide."
(*Living a Transformed Life Adequate to Our Calling*)

"To believe them, like believing anything else, means that we are set to act as if they (the 'right answers') were true, and that we will so act in appropriate circumstances. And acting as if the right answers are true means, in turn, that we intend to obey the example and teachings of Jesus our Master. What else could we intend if we believed he is who his people through the ages have declared him to be? The idea that you can trust Christ and not intend to obey him is an illusion generated by the prevalence of an unbelieving 'Christian culture.' In fact, you can no more trust Jesus and not intend to obey

126

him than you could trust your doctor or your auto mechanic and not intend to follow their advice. If you don't intend to follow their advice, you simply don't trust them." (*Living a Transformed Life Adequate to Our Calling*)

Other relevant citations

GO xi: [The] governing assumption ... the Great Disparity is firmly rooted.

See also Wilhelm Hermann, *Communion of the Christian with God*, 1909

Example—Swimming and not drowning

Imagine two youngsters learning to swim. They both dress in appropriate attire and step into the pool. They both summon their courage, take a deep breath, and duck their heads under. They both emerge coughing, having inhaled water through their noses, but want to keep going.

The first child is told by his teacher that the goal is getting across the pool without drowning. If he makes it all the way across the pool, he can go in whenever he wants to. The teacher strides to the other end of the pool, crouches down, and shouts encouragingly to the child to swim over. The child wants to be able to go into the pool whenever he wants, so though he is scared he quickly and repeatedly wiggles his arms and legs. The teacher shouts helpfully: "Reach!" "Kick!" "You can do it!" The child works hard to keep his head above water, taking in mouthfuls from time to time. Eventually the wiggles turn into a kind of dog paddle and he makes it to the other end of the pool. He's exhausted, but he has succeeded at his goal.

The second child is told that the goal is to become a strong and competent swimmer. If she becomes a good swimmer, she can go in the pool whenever she wants to. Slowly the child learns techniques for swimming. She practices keeping her face in the water and controlling her breathing. She learns to curve her fingers and stretch out her arms. She kicks efficiently from the knee. Eventually the teacher goes to the

127

other end of the pool, crouches down, and shouts encouragingly to the child to swim over. She does so easily and efficiently, emerging at the other end of the pool still rested and ready to swim some more.

Both make it to the end of the pool. Both achieve their goal of being allowed to go in any time they want. But the first child has learned to not drown; the second has learned to swim. The first child is the product of omission; the second is the product of formation.

Introduction

Holiness is a quality of likeness to God. It is a *condition* of a thing or person. Holy things are consecrated or set apart as resembling God, being inherently sacred or intended for sacred use, or both.

In the holiness code of Jewish law, there is a sense of physical separateness: something that is holy can be tainted by physical contact with something that is not. In the New Testament, something that is holy is not necessarily required to be physically separated from other things. The paradox of the Incarnation is that Jesus himself was both holy and immersed in the world.

The apostle Peter wrote to the early church: "As obedient children, do not conform to the evil desires you had when you lived in ignorance. But just as he who called you is holy, so be holy in all you do ... [having] purified yourselves by obeying the truth so that you have sincere love for each other ... (1 Peter 1:14-15, 22, NIV)" Obedience requires use of the body, mind, and will. These must be set apart to be used in a sacred manner in order for holiness to manifest, fully in the condition of the person. By being obedient to the truth, disciples do not conform to their habitual (or worldly) evil desires but, through their intentional activities, purify themselves. Their bodies become ready to do good, with their minds set on truth and their wills able to respond appropriately. This in turn develops sincere love, which itself resembles God and enables holy activity.

Definition

Holiness is a quality of likeness to God. It is a sacred condition of a thing or person, either inherently or through intention, that sets the entire thing or person apart from the common or the worldly.

129

Quotes

1.   Holiness is a quality of likeness to God.

"Holiness is not different action but different being." (*Personal notes from Fuller Seminary course GM 720, Summer 2008*)

"Holiness is, fundamentally, *otherness* or separateness from the ordinary realm of human existence in which we believe we know what we are doing and what is going on." (SD 228)

2.   It is a sacred condition of a thing or person, either inherently or through intention, that sets the entire thing or person apart from the common or the worldly.

"The salvation or deliverance of the believer in Christ is essentially holistic or whole-life." (RH 31)

"But because [the body] is holy (separated to God) we will also properly care for it: nourish, exercise, and rest it." (RH 174)

Other relevant citations

GO 62: You will consume much more grace … grace of God.

GO 90: Learning Christ-likeness … removes the readinesses to sin.

RH 174: [The] body is to be regarded … by God.

RH 220: Consequently, we do … a bodily strength that is from God.

RH 225: If God thinks fit … restore him to holiness.

SD 214: There truly is no division … to pastoral and missionary work.

HOPE

Introduction

In our cynical world, hope is sometimes ridiculed as romantic or naïve, as if anything that could be hoped for is a fantasy. Hopefulness is seen as childlike, or childish, like pretending to be a superhero or a princess. Hope itself may seem foolishly optimistic, the province of Pollyannas, and things hoped for more like wishes than possibilities.

But when the genie poofed out of Aladdin's lamp, he didn't offer to grant three hopes, but three wishes. Wishes are desires unlikely to materialize; hopes are outcomes that are happily anticipated. Hopefulness is an attitude based in confidence. This is why the writer could say, "Now faith is the assurance of things hoped for, the conviction of things not seen" (Heb. 11:1). It is also why the Spanish word for hoping (esperando) is also the word for waiting: with hope, the anticipated outcome is believed to be secure.

Definition

Hope is the confident anticipation of good. Hope deepens as our experience verifies that the object of our faith is trustworthy. The attitude of hope increasingly permeates our lives as our characters come to resemble Christ's.

Quotes

1. Hope is the confident anticipation of good.

"Fear is anticipation of evil; hope is anticipation of good." (Personal notes from the *Renovaré Institute March 2011*)

2. Hope deepens as our experience verifies that the object of our faith is trustworthy.

"Hope, the joyous expectation of those good events which our confidence in God's Rule causes us to anticipate, rises as experience of trials certifies our faith … We are saved by hope … And this hope

131

does not let us down or 'make us ashamed,' for as we live in it 'the love of God is shed abroad in our hearts by the Holy Ghost which is given unto us.' (Romans 5:5)" (*Faith, Hope and Love As Indispensable Foundations of Moral Realization*)

3.   The attitude of hope increasingly permeates our lives as our characters come to resemble Christ's.

"Romans 5:1-5 outlines an instructive and inspiring progression from an initial faith in God through Christ, with an accompanying initial hope, to a subsequent or higher-level hope that 'does not disappoint.'" (RH 129)

<u>Other relevant citations</u>

RH 129: Hope is anticipation ... what is right.

RH 130: But godly character ... life full of love.

Example—Dogs and God's kids

Well-loved dogs are generally happy. Why shouldn't they be? They are fed and housed. They are kept clean and healthy. They are praised when they do well and corrected when they err. If they were able to look ahead and fret about the future, they wouldn't, because experience would show them that they will continue to be well-loved.

A happy, healthy, well-loved dog is a hopeful dog. That dog will sidle up to you when you're not looking, and gaze at you until you pet him. He'll sit under your two-year-old's highchair, trusting she'll drop more food than she eats.

When the right time comes, the well-loved dog knows that dinner will appear. It might be late. It might be different. It might get spilled. But dinner will come. So at the right time for dinner, the well-loved dog's tail begins to wag, for it abides in hope, knowing that dinner will show up. And not just that it will show up, but that someone the dog loves will provide it.

Well-loved little children are much the same way. They abide in hope, in the deep and secure knowledge that the ones who love them will provide for them. Little children never doubt that they will be taken care of. Their bouncily excited anticipation of good things isn't wishful thinking, because they know good things will come. That is hope.

God's adult children should feel the same way. But cynicism and distrust replace hope with anxiety. Over time hope dissipates, a victim of emotional identity theft. Part of formation in Christlikeness is recognizing God's provision, reclaiming hope, and returning it to its rightful place of assuredness. Tail wagging optional.

IDENTITY

Introduction

7

With this term we have stumbled over one of the most hotly discussed (and exhaustively written about) philosophical issues of the 20th century. Since we are now in the 21st century you are free to ignore almost all of it. What you might want to notice is that Dallas uses the concept of identity in at least four distinguishable ways:

1) First, *identity* refers to the characteristic (or set of characteristics) that (perhaps uniquely) determines an individual thing or person. A simple example would be, "I knew her identity, recognizing her immediately by her voice." The main example in Dallas' work is his denial of a strong dualism. A person is not a soul that happens to be in a body; to be a particular person requires a body of some kind. Identity requires body.

2) Second, *identity* indicates the numerical singleness and unity of an object over time, as in "This is the *same* cup I used yesterday, the *identical* cup." This is what Dallas means when he talks about one's being the same (identical) person throughout eternity.

3) Third, *identity* determines a set of properties, or a close affinity, that when shared by more than one individual serves to define who that set of individuals is. For example, someone at a dog show might be concerned with the species identity of a dog: "All of these are Great Danes while all of those are Chihuahuas, but I have no idea what *that* is." Dallas used this meaning when acknowledging one's primary identity as a Christian, rather than as a Greek, Jew, woman, man, slave, free, et cetera.

4) Fourth, the concept of identity can be used to indicate the interactive relationship between the singleness of an individual and the singleness of others. Your personal identity is forged not only by your body, soul, spirit, and mind, but also through your social interactions with others who have personal identities. Their personal identities are forged through *their* bodies, souls, spirits, minds, and social interactions with you.

Definition

Identity is: 1) the characteristic (or set of characteristics) that (perhaps uniquely) determines an individual thing or person; 2) the numerical singleness and unity of an object over time; 3) a set of properties, or a close affinity, that when shared by more than one individual serves to define who that set of individuals is as a group; 4) the interaction of one's own singleness with the singleness of others.

Quotes

1.   Identity is the characteristic (or set of characteristics) that (perhaps uniquely) determines an individual thing or person.

"Who will take care of us [when we have abandoned having our own way]? The dark truth is that we may praise love ... but we do not trust love ... Above all, one has to find by thought and experience that love can be trusted as a way of life. This can be learned by interaction with Jesus in all ordinary and extraordinary circumstances ... . Love is not God, but God is love. It is who he is, his very identity. And our world under a God like that is a place where it is safe to do and be what is good and what is right." (KCT 92-93)

2.   Identity is the numerical singleness and unity of an object over time.

" ... those who love and are loved by God are not allowed to cease to exist ... He has even prepared for them an individualized eternal work in his vast universe." (DC 84)

3.   Identity determines a set of properties, or a close affinity, that when shared by more than one individual serves to define who that set of individuals is as a group

136

"[That is] what it means to be a disciple of Jesus and to be solidly committed to discipleship in their whole life. That is, when asked who they are, the first words out of their mouth would be, 'I am an apprentice of Jesus Christ.'" (RH 244)

4.   Identity is the interaction of one's own singleness with the singleness of others.

"This 'relating' quality reaches into every dimension of human existence. It characterizes the basic nature of all thought and feeling, which is always a thought of or feeling of something other than itself. It pervades the deepest reaches of our body, soul, and world, where our very identity—who we really are—is always intermingled (if sometimes negatively, by reaction) with others who have given us life, sustained us, or walked with us—or perhaps have deeply injured us. The call of 'the other' on our lives is a constant for everyone. It is the basic reality of a moral existence" (RH 183)

Other relevant citations

RH 161: ... my body is the original ... is essential to my identity.

SD 84: Human personality is not separable ... in the process of redemption.

Exercise—Clones and a fly

Notice that if you combine #1 and #2 you will be committed to the numerical singleness and unity of a person *including her body* over time. The question of identity then becomes: how much change can a body have before it stops being the one body of a unique person? Several movies play with this idea, among them 1986's *The Fly*, in which the body of a scientist comes to resemble that of a fly. Along with the changes in his body come alterations in his emotions, physical needs and desires, and interactions with others. When does he stop being that scientist or individual person? Stop being a man (and start being a fly)?

137

In 1996's *Mulitiplicity*, a man gets repeatedly cloned to deal with his overscheduled life. This movie addresses the distinction between #1 and #3 above: which of the (cloned or original) men is the "real" one, or do they all equally share an identity?

While these concerns are not terribly relevant to understanding Dallas' books, they do make for pleasant puzzling!

INNER REALITY

Introduction

We know that what we notice through our physical senses is a mere whisper compared to the totality of God, the universe, and everything else. Yet it is easy to unthinkingly interpret what we see as the whole of reality. If a driver crosses three lanes of traffic and exits the highway, we are likely to attribute character traits, intentions, abilities, even ethical standards to the driver. If we notice someone doing something well, we may think the activity is easy for him, or that he has natural talent, or enjoys doing it. Recognizing that what we see is not all there is, Jesus referred to the religious authorities as "whitewashed tombs" (Mt. 23:27): clean and beautiful on the outside, dead and filthy on the inside. The apostle Paul noted in himself that his desire for goodness and the activities of his body weren't always in alignment—his good desires weren't all there is (Rom. 7:22-24).

Clearly the inner reality and the outer expression or activity of a person can be quite different. In truth, our external reality is far less affected by God: more often than not it is our thinking, emotions, ideas, impulses, and such things that are touched by the Holy Spirit, rather than our elbows or houses. And if there is any immediate substantial change in us at baptism or rebirth, it is not in the tangible aspects of our lives: we become "part of the vine" on the *inside*. Since it is possible to change what our bodies do without transforming our inner reality, the focus of spiritual formation must be on changing our inner reality.

{*Definition follows on next page.*}

Definition

The inner reality of the self is the location of spiritual transformation and of one's identity in Jesus. This inner reality includes thoughts, feelings, desires, will, continuity of experience, memory, and so forth. Inner reality may include any aspect of the person that is not strictly bodily or social, though one's inner reality is affected by both the body and the social environment, and the inner reality effects activity in the body and the social environment.

Quotes

"The outcome of spiritual formation is, indeed, the transformation of the inner reality of the self in such a way that the deeds and words of Jesus become a natural expression of who we are. But it is the nature of the human being that the 'inner reality of the self' settles into our body, from which that inner reality then operates in practice." (RH 165)

"Spiritual transformation into Christlikeness, I have said, is the process of forming the inner world of the human self in such a way that it takes on the character of the inner being of Jesus himself. The result is that the 'outer' life of the individual increasingly becomes a natural expression of the inner reality of Jesus and of his teachings. Doing what he said and did increasingly becomes a part of who we are. (RH 159)

Other relevant citations

DC 25-26: Thus, contrary to a popular idea … the whole of the physical universe.

DC 279: The personal presence of Jesus … can its absence.

INTENTION

Introduction

Let us say that for the sake of your health you intend to work out at the gym today. Does that mean a) you are compelled to work out and cannot fail to do so; b) you know when it fits into your schedule but you may not make it; or c) you think you would like to go? If you are using the word "intention" the way most of us do, your answer is somewhere between b and c. That is, you have a vision of what you want (health), you have a goal (working out at the gym), and you have means (time in your schedule and a way to get there), but it is far from certain that you will actually follow through. So what might be holding you back even though you intend to go? What does having an intention really mean?

For human beings, intention is much more closely connected to vision and goals than to action. Humans do not have complete control over our wills, or our thoughts, feelings, desires, and bodies, for that matter. It is quite possible for you to have a vision of some wonderful state of affairs or some goal and have no intention of bringing it about. You can have the vision of a goal and the intention to achieve it, but never actually find the means to fulfill the intention. You can have the vision, intention and means yet never take the action that would fulfill the intention and effect the vision: you might get to the end of your day and realize you didn't actually get to the gym.

If we intend something, we must also *decide* to move ahead on the intention—perhaps re-deciding on a regular basis—and have the *means* and instrumentalities to carry it out, along with the *vision* to sustain the intention and an extended effort.

Definition

Intention is the purposeful willing toward activity that is presumed to be able to achieve a desired end. Whatever God intends is already in the process of coming to fruition.

Quotes

"Now, an intention is whole and real only if it includes a decision to fulfill or carry through with the intention. We commonly find people who say they intend (or intended) to do certain things that they do not do. To be fair, external circumstances may sometimes have prevented them from carrying out the action. And habits deeply rooted in our bodies and life contexts can, for a while, thwart even a sincere intention. But if something like that is not the case, we know that they never actually decided to do what they say they intended to do, and that they therefore did not really intend to do it. Accordingly they lack the power and order that intention brings into life processes." (*Living a Transformed Life Adequate to Our Calling*)

Other relevant citations

DC 379: [T]he intention of God ... for his children.

GO 85: Intention alone cannot suffice ... life in the Spirit.

GO 124: It is God's intention ... fruit of the Spirit.

RH 83: We must intend the vision ... to reality.

RH 87-89: Concretely, we intend to live ... that trust in him takes .... Then the vision ... and character.

RH 244: If spiritual formation ... their group.

Example—Reason 47a for why we are not God

As the Apostle Paul lamented, our will and our desire don't always match up. To make matters worse, our desire and will may be working together while our bodily habits battle against both of them. Take biting your nails, or any other nervous habit, as an example: you can suddenly realize you're nibbling them to nubs at the same time your will is racing to leave them alone.

But God's will is utterly under God's control; God never suddenly realizes that his body has been doing something he never intended. Moreover, God's power is completely aligned with God's willing: if God wills something, it happens at the moment of willing. That means that for God, vision, intention, and decision are one conjoined activity. If God has a vision of a goal, by virtue of its being a *goal* God must have the intention of bringing it about. For God to have the vision and intention indicates a pre-existing or concurrent decision to bring it about.

Because of all this, if God intends something, the effectuation of that is already in process. But not with us: we need vision, intention, means, and decision to get anything of import done.

Introduction

Unlike happiness, which is a transitory feeling, joy is an overall sensibility. Joy is a deep-seated sense of well-being, of ultimate safety in the universe. Joy is not triggered by external events or by internal impetus, and so is not crushed by them either: the world cannot give you joy and it cannot take it away. Instead, joy is the normal product of a life lived in love. It is a character trait developed by grace and effort as part of the fruit of the Spirit. God is joyful, and as we come to resemble Christ, our joy fills.

> ### Definition
>
> Joy is a deep-seated sense of well-being, of safety in God's universe. Joy is part of the fruit of the Spirit, growing as a natural product of the transformation of one's inner self to be like that of Christ, which itself is full of joy.

Quotes

1. Joy is a deep-seated sense of well-being, of safety in God's universe.

Joy is natural in the presence of such love. Joy is a pervasive sense-not just a thought-of well-being: of overall and ultimate well-being. Its primary feeling component is delight in an encompassing good well-secured. (RH 132)

2. Joy is part of the fruit of the Spirit ...

"The fruit of the Spirit simply is the inner character of Jesus himself that is brought about in us through the process of Christian spiritual formation. It is the outcome of spiritual formation. It is 'Christ formed in us.' ... we have received the presence of Christ's Spirit through the process of spiritual formation, and now that Spirit, interacting with us, fills us with love, joy, peace ...." (GO 115)

3.   … growing as a natural product of the transformation of one's inner self to be like that of Christ, …

"Joy is a basic element of inner transformation into Christlikeness and of the outer life that flows from it." (RH 133)

"[One main part of developing disciples is to] form the insights and habits of the student's mind so that it stays directed toward God. When this is adequately done, a full heart of love will go out toward God, and joy and obedience will flood the life." (DC 325)

4.   … [Christ's inner self] itself is full of joy.

"We should, to begin with, think that God leads a very interesting life, and that he is full of joy. Undoubtedly he is the most joyous being in the universe. The abundance of his love and generosity is inseparable from his infinite joy. All of the good and beautiful things from which we occasionally drink tiny droplets of soul-exhilarating joy, God continuously experiences in all their breadth and depth and richness." (DC 62)

Other relevant citations

DC 378: Thus, our faithfulness … in all its dimensions.

RH 128: When we properly cultivate … joy, and peace.

RH 132: [In] joy, all is well … loss it may involve.

RH 133: Having one's joy "full" … (Nehemiah 8:10, PAR).

Example—Down in your heart

Do you know the children's song that goes, "I've got the joy joy joy joy down in my heart"? The four "joy"s in that first line may alert you that, like most kids' songs, it's pretty repetitive. It continues with "Down in my heart, down in my heart," and finishes with "down in my heart to stay." Compare that song with "If you're happy and you know it, clap your hands," which reminds the singer that if you are happy, your face will show it. Later in the song you stomp your feet if you're happy, but it's still your face that gives you away.

These are simple songs, but they convey a deeper truth: happiness comes from the outside and is expressed there; joy lives deep in the heart.

JUSTIFICATION

Introduction

Justification is the first step of three in the classical doctrine of the process of salvation; the other two are sanctification and glorification. Justification is the forgiveness of sins and the regeneration of the soul, along with an attendant assurance of everlasting life in the presence of God. Theologians disagree about the mechanism of justification, that is, exactly what *about* Jesus' life and death and glorification makes justification available to human beings. Where they agree is that justification is an action of grace God takes in response to one's faith.

Regeneration, which is a part of justification, is when a believer is reborn, receiving a literal new life through the impartation of Christ. It is the regeneration of a person that makes it possible for her or him to access the kingdom of heaven and to become Christlike.

The reason all this classical theology matters is that in the past decades, the entire concept of salvation has been flattened into just another word for justification, and a pretty thin justification at that. Even the concept of being *born again* has been stripped of its reality, the phrase becoming synonymous with *being saved*. In this flattening of salvation, regeneration—the literal new life—is omitted from justification.

So when people ask, "are you saved?" what they are often asking is "have you accepted a particular formulation of faith in Jesus, so that you can go to heaven when you die?" Salvation is equated with going to heaven, which seems to be all there is to being a Christian. This is the background problem for what Dallas termed *the great omission*: the loss of any perceived need for discipleship or transformation in the life of the Christian.

[Definition follows on next page.]

Definition

Justification is the act of God that forgives our sin and enables everlasting life in God's presence. Within justification is an instantaneous occurrence of regeneration or rebirth, in which we are given a new self that is capable of Christlikeness. It is a part of the process of salvation, rather than the end of it.

Quotes

"I would say that justification is a new beginning for a relationship that has been broken, and it is made right by forgiveness, but that's just the doorway into the resumption of relationship." (Dallas Willard, quoted by Gary W. Moon in "Getting the Elephant Out of the Sanctuary," *Conversations Journal* 8.1, Spring/Summer 2010.)

"We have to deal with a massive population of churched and unchurched people who think of 'being saved' or 'being right with God' merely in terms of some picture of justification, not regeneration. Being 'born again' is usually understood now, not in terms of being animated by a 'life from above,' but in terms of a profession of faith—often a profession of faith in the death of Christ as bearing the punishment for sin that otherwise would fall on us. This understanding usually prevails in ways that do not involve—may not even make mention of—participation in divine life. (And, of course, one can mention it without engaging it.) Then, of course, the otherwise natural progression into discipleship and its spiritual (trans)formation naturally does not occur, and the churches and surrounding society is flooded with discipleshipless Christians whose lives seem not to differ profoundly, if at all, from non-Christians." (*Spiritual Formation As a Natural Outcome of Salvation*)

"The steamship whose machinery is broken may be brought into port and made fast to the dock. She is safe, but not sound. Repairs may last a long time. Christ designs to make us both safe and sound.

Justification gives the first—safety; sanctification gives the second—soundness." (RH 225, quoting an unknown author)

"[Justification is] absolutely vital, for our sins have to be forgiven. But justification is not something separable from regeneration. And regeneration naturally moves into sanctification and glorification." (GO 62)

Other relevant citations

John Wesley, Sermon 45: The New Birth

John Calvin, *Institutes of Religion* Book III, Chapters 3, 11, 14

KINGDOM OF God

Introduction

Ever hear the phrase, "A man's home is his castle"? Written in a time when castles were more common, this actually comes from English common law, and was written in 1628 by Sir Edward Coke as "a man's house is his castle" to define the realm over which a man had reign.

Dallas wrote that one's kingdom is the range of one's effective will. To put it another way, the word *kingdom* may be read as "the realm over which one reigns." In whatever aspect of your life you have the deciding voice, that aspect is part of your kingdom: you reign over it. Individuals have larger or smaller kingdoms, depending upon what we control or influence. Warren Buffett probably has a larger kingdom than you do, and you have a larger kingdom than a slave, who may not have sovereignty even over her own body. God has the largest kingdom of all, for wherever God has the final say in a matter, that is his kingdom.

God allows individuals to have kingdoms; that is the source of our freedom. Because of this kingdoms clash: ours against another's, ours against God's. But God's goal is that we will place our kingdom under the influence of God's kingdom. We retain our sovereignty, but maintain deference to the larger kingdom. In other words, we do what we want, but what we want is in line with what God wants.

To live in the kingdom of God requires bringing our personal kingdoms into God's kingdom, placing them under submission to God as ultimate sovereign.

Definition

A kingdom is area of life over which one has the deciding voice; it is where one's will is done. As a result, kingdoms clash as the will of one bumps up against the will of another. God's intent is that we mesh our kingdoms with each other, under the sovereign rule of God's kingdom.

Quotes

1. A kingdom is area of life over which one has the deciding voice; it is where one's will is done.

"To gain deeper understanding of our eternal kind of life in God's present kingdom, we must be sure to understand what a *kingdom* is. Every last one of us has a 'kingdom'—or 'queendom,' or a 'government'—a realm that is uniquely our own, where our choice determines what happens .... Our 'kingdom' is simply *the range of our effective will.* Whatever we genuinely have the say over is *in* our kingdom. And our having the say over something is precisely what places it within our kingdom." (DC 21)

"My body is the original and primary place of my dominion and my responsibility." (RH 161)

2. As a result, kingdoms clash as the will of one bumps up against the will of another.

"In developing my dominion I soon run into realities that do not yield to my will. Often these are the kingdoms of other individuals, organized around their desires and contrary to my own." (RH 161)

3. God's intent is that we mesh our kingdoms with each other, under the sovereign rule of God's kingdom.

"His intent is for us to learn to mesh our kingdom with the kingdoms of others. Love of neighbor, rightly understood, will make this happen. But we can only love adequately by taking as our primary aim the integration of our rule with God's. That is why love of

154

neighbor is the second, not the first, commandment ... Only as we find that kingdom and settle into it can we human beings *all* reign, or rule, together with God. We will then enjoy individualized 'reigns' with neither isolation nor conflict." (DC 26)

"Giving is, among other things, an exercise in turning loose of what we have in our little 'kingdom' to enter into the amazing reciprocity that God has built into the human heart." (KCT 160)

Other relevant citations

DC 29: One thing that may mislead us ... God's present rule on earth.

RH 161: From one essential perspective ... can we extend our "kingdom."

Example—The union of kingdoms in marriage

Usually interpreted as referring to marriage, the gospel according to Matthew states that "the two will become one flesh." It is perhaps significant that Matthew did not write, "the two will become one will." Anyone who has ever been married knows that *that* is not true: wills clash all the time in every significant relationship, including marriage. Where wills clash, there is a conflict between kingdoms. Where they align, there is a unity between kingdoms.

This is clearer when you think of the kings and queens of history. A kingdom is the area over which a king's word is treated as law. There used to be only a couple of ways for a king to enlarge his territory, mainly war and strategic marriage. So when Isabella of Castille married Ferdinand of Aragon, their realms were united. Isabella ruled Castille, Ferdinand ruled Aragon, but together they laid the groundwork for Spain.

The same is true in marriage. Two people join their reigns—the areas of their lives over which they have final say—into a single unity, while retaining the right of rule over part. Marriages work when the two rulers practice mutual submission, in deference to the benefit of their united kingdoms.

KINGDOM LIVING

Introduction

The gospel of Jesus is the "good news of the presence and availability of life in the kingdom, now and forever, through reliance on Jesus the Anointed." (DC 49) Dallas proclaimed this gospel through his work of envisioning God's kingdom, expressing its qualities, sharing the means to live in it now, and articulating God's intention to have us reign in it forever. *Kingdom living* or *life in the kingdom* is shorthand for all of that: vision, qualities, means, and God's intention for us in it.

Be careful, then, that in reading *kingdom living* or *life in the kingdom* you do not truncate the meaning, making it a term designating specific activities or attitudes. Living in the kingdom is not an add-on to salvation, the end goal of the future Second Coming, or a defined set of daily activities. It is, rather, the point of everything.

Definition

Kingdom living is a term for the qualities associated with living under the reign of God in one's own life now and forever. One enters into kingdom living through a transforming relationship with Jesus which begins, and perhaps remains, one of apprenticeship to the master of this kind of life.

Quotes

1. Kingdom living is a term for the qualities associated with living under the reign of God in one's own life now and forever.

"What we are aiming for in this vision is to live fully in the kingdom of God and as fully as possible now and here, not just hereafter." (RH 86)

"My first step then, 'as I go,' is to be his disciple, and constantly to be learning from him how to live my life in the Kingdom of God now—my real life, the one I am actually living." (GO 226)

"For those who do so seek and find it in Christ, it is true even now that 'all things work together for their good' (Romans 8:28, PAR), and that nothing can cut them off from God's inseparable love and effective care (Romans 8:35-39). That is the nature of a life in the kingdom of the heavens now." (*Living a Transformed Life Adequate to Our Calling*)

"Our aim in such a life is to identify all that we are and all that we do with God's purposes in creating us and our world ... .This is the life beyond, and yet inclusive of, his guiding word. It is the life that has its beginning in the additional birth and its culmination in the everlasting, glorious society of heaven." (HG 211)

2.   One enters into kingdom living through a transforming relationship with Jesus which begins, and perhaps remains, one of apprenticeship to the master of this kind of life.

"To be a disciple is to be an apprentice or student of Jesus in Kingdom living." (GO 166)

"And how can I become a genuinely good person? (By being a faithful apprentice of Jesus in Kingdom living, learning from him how to live my life as he would live my life if he were I.)" (GO 219-20)

Other relevant citations

DC 64: It is deeply illuminating ... even grief. (DC 64)

KCT 152: Entering the kingdom ... and hour by hour.

RH 86: The vision that underlies ... in our lifetime on earth.

RH 87: The vision of life ... no way to enter it.

RH 109: Am I undertaking some task? ... the fulfillment of his purposes."

RH 132: The fellowship ... (John 13:34-35).

RH 244: If spiritual formation is to be ... the basic good news ...

Example—The kingdom lifestyle

From 1984 to 1995, American television watchers wallowed in the extravagant "Lifestyles of the Rich and Famous." In 1994 the Sacramento band Cake released a song that described someone's expensive, dissolute, and drug-addled daily life as his "rock'n'roll lifestyle." We casually refer to the "gay lifestyle," the "vegan lifestyle," and the "suburban lifestyle," among too many others. Obviously there is a problem with this kind of generalizing, since the vegan who lives in rural India will have a very different life than that of celebrity Ellen DeGeneres, who is also vegan. Moreover, lifestyles overlap, so one could conceivably have a gay rock'n'roll lifestyle, a wealthy suburban vegan lifestyle, and so forth. But the idea is that through whatever it is the members of a community share in common—wealth, rock and roll, living in a suburb, being gay, or practicing veganism—a way of life emerges, and with it an identifiable common lifestyle.

Now imagine a large group of people, spread across countries and continents, whose single commonality is a transforming relationship with some person, say, Jesus. As the relationship grows, their way of life is transformed to resemble his. As their way of life comes to look like his way of life, an identifiable lifestyle will emerge, based on the defining aspect of his way of life. Dallas might have said that the defining aspect of Jesus' way of life (his Way) was constant immersion in the will, power, and presence of God, i.e. God's reign or kingdom. Thus whatever comes out of constant immersion in the will, power, and presence of God is the lifestyle of the group. Dallas described the kingdom lifestyle as living my life as Jesus would live my life if he were I.

A random note: the Cake CD that contained "Rock'n'Roll Lifestyle" also held "Jesus Wrote A Blank Check," in which the singer worries that he won't get around to kingdom living before it's too late.

Kingdom of God

THE KINGDOM OF THE HEAVENS

Introduction 7

Dallas used *kingdom of the heavens* and *kingdom of God* interchangeably, noting in *The Divine Conspiracy* C.H. Dodd's opinion that they are synonymous (DC 73). Occasionally he referred to the *kingdom among us* to emphasize God's dwelling presence in human experience.

The simple definition derives from the meaning of *kingdom*, that is, the realm over which one reigns. The kingdom of the heavens, then, is the realm over which God reigns, or as Dallas usually phrased it, "the range of God's effective will," though it might be said that in its simplicity this definition loses the power of the concept.

The kingdom of the heavens is where God is interactively and creatively present, and where those who are also present respond to God's will. Look at the breadth of that statement! Biblically, the heavens are not out there somewhere, beyond space and time, waiting for humans to arrive. The heavens are the entire universe, both out of space and time and in them. The heavens are local, for wherever God is the heavens are, and God is local. The kingdom of the heavens was *always* present throughout the physical and spiritual cosmos; Jesus simply made it *accessible* to us.

Kingdom of the heavens is not simply a political designation, describing only the functional limits of a particular sovereign state. The kingdom of the heavens encompasses the range of God's effective will *and* the qualities of the kingdom in which God's will reigns.

[*Definition follows on next page.*]

Definition

The kingdom of the heavens (*or* of God) is the range of God's effective will, hence anything that obeys God's will is within his kingdom. It has always existed, but has been made accessible to everyone through Jesus Christ.

The term *kingdom of the heavens* includes all the qualities that living under the rule of a sovereign, loving, creative Trinitarian God implies. *The kingdom among us*, which refers to the same thing, specially emphasizes God's presence in and among those over whom he reigns.

Quotes

1.   The kingdom of the heavens (*or* of God) is the range of God's effective will, hence anything that obeys God's will is within his kingdom.

"God's own 'kingdom,' or 'rule,' is the range of his effective will, where what he wants done is done. The person of God himself and the action of his will are the organizing principles of his kingdom, but everything that obeys those principles, whether by nature or by choice, is *within* his kingdom … . [T]hat kingdom has existed from the moment of creation and will never end. It cannot be 'shaken' and is totally good. It has never been in trouble and never will be. It is not something that human beings produce or, ultimately, can hinder …. Accordingly, the kingdom of God is not essentially a social or political reality at all. Indeed, the social and political realm, along with the individual heart, is the only place in all of creation where the kingdom of God, or his effective will, is currently permitted to be absent … . Thus, contrary to a popular idea, the kingdom of God is not *primarily* something that is 'in the hearts of men.' … It is not some matter or inner attitude or faith that might be totally disconnected from the public, behavioral, visible world. It always pervades and governs the whole of the physical universe." (DC 25-26)

162

2.   It has always existed, but has been made accessible to everyone through Jesus Christ.

"[Jesus] came proclaiming access to the kingdom of God: to God's present care and supervision, available to all through confidence in himself." (RH 67)

3.   The term *kingdom of the heavens* includes all the qualities that living under the rule of a sovereign, loving, creative Trinitarian God implies.

"[The] kingdom come in its utter fullness … peace as wholeness, as fullness of function, as the restful but unending creativity involved in a cosmoswide, cooperative pursuit of a created order that continuously approaches but never reaches the limitless goodness and greatness of the triune personality of God, its source." (DC 400)

"[The] Kingdom of God is so gentle that as long as we're acting, it usually just lets us go on." (GO 176)

4.   *The kingdom among us,* which refers to the same thing, specially emphasizes God's presence in and among those over whom he reigns.

"To be born 'from above,' in New Testament language, means to be interactively joined with a dynamic, unseen system of divine reality in the midst of which all of humanity moves about—whether it knows it or not. And that, of course, is 'The Kingdom Among Us.'" (DC 68)

Other relevant citations

DC 11: God's desire … is a community of boundless and totally competent love.

DC 130: [Jesus'] overall picture … is perfect and whole.

DC 182: [In agape love] we achieve living union … 1 Corinthians 13.

DC 208: What is most valuable … will last forever.

DC 283-84: [He] lives in the kingdom of God … live my life if he were I.

GO xiv: Eternal life is … through apprenticeship to Jesus.

GO 178-79: Finding the Kingdom of God ... to interact with God there.

Exercise—In your car as it is in the heavens

In some times and places we find it easy to experience the kingdom of the heavens, that is, to obey God, to recognize God's activity, to find rest in God's presence. In other times and places? Not so much.

Imagine for a moment your most consistently un-kingdom-like location or activity. Maybe when you are driving you are likely to live outside God's kingdom. Maybe it's when you're working at your job. Maybe when your kid is being belligerent and bratty you find it hard to manage kingdom living. Whatever it is, imagine that.

©alvinmann

Add to that picture of the un-kingdom God's loving reign permeating the activity or place. Saturating it. Imagine God's joyously boundless and totally competent love pouring through your car, or job, or kid's room. This is the meaning of "on earth as it is in the heavens," where we pray that God's will be done.

Next time someone tailgates you, remember: in my car as it is in the heavens.

164

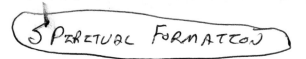

KNOWING CHRIST

Introduction

Common sense tells us that to know *about* something is not the same as *knowing* it. The guy who knows *about* brain surgery, even one who has extensive breadth of information about technique and application, is not the one you want operating on your brain.

This difference between knowing *about* and knowing is crucial when it comes to kingdom living. Knowing about Jesus, or even trusting that what you know about Jesus is true, isn't going to get you the quality of life with God that he had. Even a higher form of acquaintance—knowing that Jesus is "Lord and Savior" or that he "died for your sins"—isn't the same as knowing Jesus. It might be enough for a minimal version of justification—forgiveness and a ticket to heaven—but knowing *about* Jesus, even attributing power and importance to him, simply isn't what is required for that certain kind of life.

Living in the kind of relationship with God that Jesus had requires more than knowing *about* Jesus. It's like getting to know anything. You get to know a skill (like brain surgery) with your hands on. You get to know a person by spending extensive time with him, listening, talking, following, watching, arguing, eating—living life with him.

Doing all this changes you. In the case of knowing Jesus, your inner self is gradually transformed to be more like his, which means that you gradually live more fully like him, which is more fully in the kingdom of God.

Definition

Ţo know Christ is to be in an increasingly interactive relationship with him, experiencing his presence and his way of living, that transforms your way of life to be more like his, which is life in the kingdom of God.

Quotes

"Knowledge 'at a distance,' knowing certain 'facts' about something, doesn't amount to knowing *it*. It therefore does not have the same power over life …. The way of Jesus Christ is a way of *firsthand interaction* … you can't really sustain a kingdom life, a life 'not of this world, without such interaction with the King. And such an interaction with God is the most precious thing available to any human being. It simply *is* eternal life." (KCT 141-42)

"Knowledge in biblical language never refers to what we today call 'head knowledge,' but always to experiential involvement with what is known—to actual engagement with it." (RH 50)

Other relevant citations

KCT 67: If you really want to know Christ now … up to the present.

KCT 147-48: To come to know [Christ] … can lead them into increasing knowledge of him.

KCT 152: [To] know Christ in the kingdom of God … that is trust in Christ.

Example—Parachuting into Africa

You might listen to how you talk about knowing people. Acquaintances reckon one kind of voice: "Yeah, I know him." Friends—especially those who may have done something wrong—get another kind: "That can't be. I KNOW him!" In fact, we may scorn those who intimate that they deeply know someone with whom they have a passing acquaintance, calling them "name-droppers," or "social climbers." Somehow this automatic distinction got lost when it comes to Jesus.

Imagine that your Kenyan neighbor has told you all about Kenya and her life there. That may be all she ever talks about, so much and so often you feel as though you know everything about her home country. Would you say you *know* Kenya? That is, if you parachuted into Nairobi at two in the morning onto an empty street, would you feel confident that you knew the city, country, customs, and language well enough to build a new life there?

You get to know a place by immersing yourself in it, walking its streets, hanging out with its people. It's the same with knowing Christ: if you're not immersing yourself in his presence, doing what he does, talking over things with him, you might find that you're really just name-dropping.

Introduction

We encounter three main issues in Dallas' use of the word *knowledge*. First is distinguishing knowledge from other kinds of mental activity, such as belief, faith, opinion, observation, and so forth. Second is acknowledging there is such a thing as knowledge of non-material or non-sensual substances. Third is understanding the biblical idea of knowledge as interactive experience.

All these aspects of knowledge rest on two particular assumptions: reality exists and can be investigated. To say that reality exists is to say that there *is* a "there" independent of your conceptual schemes: reality isn't just in your head. That reality can be investigated and apprehended.

Dallas held one other important assumption about reality: it is not limited to material, spacial, or sensible objects. The objects of reality may also be non-material, non-spacial, and not directly available to investigation by the senses. Knowledge of non-material reality comes about through different methods of investigation than that of material reality. For something material, like a table, touch can impart knowledge. For something non-material, like contempt, or spiritual, like God, touch will not be an appropriate tool for gaining knowledge.

Notice that knowing a person is different than knowing about a person. Knowledge about a person is gained through acquisition of data. Knowledge of a person is gained through interactive relationship. When *knowledge* appears in the Bible, it refers to the kind of thing gained by interactive relationship.

Definition

Knowledge is accurate representation of reality, when that representation is based on some combination of authority, reason and experience. Accurate representation of non-material or non-sensual reality, based on some combination of authority, reason and experience, is possible.

Knowledge, in the biblical sense, is interactive experience – knowledge *of* rather than knowledge *about*.

Quotes

1.   Knowledge is accurate representation of reality, when that representation is based on some combination of authority, reason and experience.

"We have knowledge of something when we are representing it (thinking about it, speaking of it, treating it) as it actually is, on an appropriate basis of thought and experience." (KCT 15)

"Knowledge, but not mere belief or commitment, confers on its possessor an authority or right—even a responsibility—to act ... because knowledge involves truth: truth secured by experience, method, and evidence that is generally available." (KCT 17-18)

2.   Accurate representation of non-material or non-sensual reality, based on some combination of authority, reason and experience, is possible.

"[K]nowledge of the nonphysical source of the physical universe is possible to those who will invest *due diligence* concerning the matter ... To understand the basic character of the physical world is, we have pointed out, to be in a position to know that is has a nonphysical source ... But one way of *not* knowing what is quite knowable is to refuse to think matters out to the end ... in a carefully attentive and thorough manner." (KCT 108-09)

170

"Empiricism as a theory of knowledge is a recognized failure in any form that has been definitely specified, and has nothing left to support it but the bias of a sensualistic culture. There is no reason to regard conclusions about mind or substance that derive from it as serious challenges to what the ordinary, thoughtful and experienced person assumes to be the case about self-knowledge and self-identity. Anything that we can accurately report about our experience must be assumed to be the case, and there are a huge number of things of various general types that any individual can accurately report about their own minds and experience." (*On the Texture and Substance of the Human Soul*)

3.   Knowledge, in the biblical sense, is interactive experience—knowledge *of* rather than knowledge *about*.

"What we see [in the centurion's response to Jesus] is trust based upon experiential knowledge of the power in the words spoken by authorized individuals." (HG 129)

"Knowledge in biblical language never refers to what we today call 'head knowledge,' but always to experiential involvement with what is known—to actual engagement with it." (RH 50)

Other relevant citations

GO 140: We have knowledge of a subject matter when ... evaluate authorities.

KCT 7-8: [There] is a body of uniquely Christian knowledge ... suited to its subject matter.

KCT 9: Western intellectual history shows ... have been proved to be false.

KCT 18: Belief and knowledge are different kinds of things ... we know.

KCT 19: Ideally, knowledge is ... and perhaps it is mere profession.

KCT 141: Knowledge "at a distance," ... direct awareness of him and his kingdom.

See also Dallas' articles, "A Crucial Error in Epistemology", "Finding the Noema" *and* "Knowledge", *available at dwillard.org.*

LAW

Introduction

Some Christians have been taught three things about biblical law: 1) it's all written out in the first five books of the Old Testament (or *Torah* or *Pentateuch*), mostly in Leviticus; 2) it doesn't apply since Jesus came along; and 3) observing laws leads to sin while following the Holy Spirit doesn't. Even though Jesus said that he didn't come to abolish the law (Mt. 5:17), and Paul spent much of Romans 2 and 3 explaining and justifying the role of law in the lives of Christians, we can still get it very wrong.

When the Bible refers to the law, it does not mean the 613 rules found in Torah. The law of the God of Israel is the written and oral collection of fundamental teachings given to Israel, including (but not limited to) the Ten Commandments (Ex. 20:1-17) , the Shema (Deut. 6:4-5), the Leviticus passage on neighbor love (19:9-8), and the word of the prophets concerning the law. The law as it is articulated is a reflection of the reality of God's orderly universe.

Thus one can obey the law without resorting to either legalism or rigid adherence to a list of shalts and shalt nots. It is legalism that leads to sin, not obedience. Indeed, knowledge of and obedience to the law shapes and restores the soul. The law is, therefore, a grace of God.

The law of the God of Israel has not been set aside by Jesus; Jesus provides the means to fulfill the law. By living in the kingdom of God, according to the reality and rhythms of God, Jesus obeys the covenant law given to Israel and the "royal law of love" that undergirds it.

It is the content of his character and the wholeness of his soul that enable his easy obedience. The means he provides for a life within the law is the intentional shaping of character, commonly known as spiritual formation. When we live as he lived, our character being transformed in Christlikeness, we will also obey the law.

Definition

Law is the grace-filled orderly reality "behind" the written law that powerfully redeems and restores the soul. The "royal law of love" is the formulation (found in the Old Testament and articulated in oral Torah but recapitulated by Jesus) that encompasses all the law but preferences love (Luke 10:27). Character shaping through intentional spiritual formation and the grace of God makes possible easy adherence to the law of God.

Quotes

1.   Law is the grace-filled orderly reality "behind" the written law that powerfully redeems and restores the soul.

"[Love] of the law restores the soul. Law is good for the soul, is an indispensable instrument of instruction and a standard of judgment of good and evil. Walking in the law with God restores the soul because the law expresses the order of God's kingdom and of God's own character." (RH 215)

2.   The *royal law of love* is the formulation (found in the Old Testament and articulated in oral Torah but recapitulated by Jesus) that encompasses all the law but preferences love (Luke 10:27).

"The correct order that the soul requires for its vitality and proper functioning is found in the 'royal law' of love (James 2:8), abundantly spelled out in Jesus and his teaching. That law includes all that was essential in the older law, which he fulfilled and enables us to fulfill through constant discipleship to him." (RH 215)

"Moral rules are subordinate to the moral attitude or disposition of love … . law is not sufficient for love … You can keep the law as divinely formulated *without* loving your neighbor or even yourself." (KCT 90)

3.   Character shaping through intentional spiritual formation and the grace of God allows easy adherence to the law of God.

174

"[When] we bring the reflective will to life in Christ (birth 'from above'), and add the instruction of the law and the presence of the Holy Spirit, along with the fellowship of his Body, we have the wherewithal to live in such a way that God is glorified in everything we do." (*Spiritual Formation and the Warfare Between the Flesh and the Human Spirit*)

"[We] cannot keep the law by trying to keep the law. To succeed in keeping the law one must aim at something other and something more. One must aim to become the *kind of person* from whom the deeds of the law naturally flow." (DC 142-43)

Other relevant citations

DC 141-42: God's law is ... drink in his power.

DC 142: A time will come in human history ... the deliverance of humankind in history and beyond.

RH 211: The law of the Lord gratefully received ... and redemptively.

RH 212: Spirit, covenant, and law ... one who walks with God.

RH 214: The presence of the Spirit ... righteousness in terms of actions.

RH 215: The law is ... kingdom of God.

RH 215: [There] is much more to the law ... his creation.

Example—Teaching kids the rules

The relationship between the written laws, the reality behind the law, and the spirit of the law is never clearer than when you are trying to teach kids The Rules. If you're teaching them well, eventually your kids have absorbed The Rules and obey them without referring to any physical or mental list.

The Rules are not the rules of life or of baseball or even of your house. The Rules are the boundaries and behaviors that you expect kids to respect whether you tell them what to do or not. Maybe you want your teenager to call if he's going to be late, not because it's a law (with punishment for its breach), but because he is the kind of kid who knows you'll be worried and doesn't want to worry you unnecessarily. If he does that, he has actually learned The Rules.

Teaching The Rules to kids looks a lot like the history of the law of the God of Israel: When kids are very young, they don't have many rules, but the ones they have are critical: don't eat poison or jump off the roof. When human beings were still new, they didn't have many either, really just *trust God* and *don't eat the fruit of that tree.*

As kids get older, they have to play with other kids and learn from adults. Those old critical rules still stand, but they get others, mostly to guide their interactions. *Don't kill each other. Pay your debts. Let people off the hook. Honor your elders.*

At the same time you're teaching them those rules of interaction, you're telling them stories that begin "when I was your age," and allowing them to get pushed down once in a while. *"Remember the wonders he has done, his miracles, and the judgments he pronounced." "They will sow wheat but reap thorns; they will wear themselves out but gain nothing."* Through repetition you build into them habits of behavior and thought that make the lists of rules less important.

As they get older still, you give them more freedom to make mistakes and more responsibility. They learn from their actions more than your admonitions, but if all goes well, all those little rules and stories and consequences and mistakes shape them into the kind of people who just do the right thing. When they don't, they have to learn the laws again. And again.

In the end, obedience to The Rules is a matter of character, not of law, and good character is shaped by interaction with someone who has good character.

176

LIFE

Introduction

Life is the essential concept in Dallas' work. That can be pretty unusual for a professional philosopher, even a theologian, because academia tends to value abstractions, and real life is anything but abstract.

The "realness" of life doesn't lend itself to easy discussion, and the word itself is rich with layers of meaning and uses, such as:

Life, as in being alive (and not dead);

Life, as a quality of understanding (as in what choices and ideas are "living" and accessible);

Life in the spirit (or "in Jesus", or "in him");

Life from above (and not from physical birth);

Life under the reign of God (rather than under our own reign);

Life, as in daily activity (what we do with our days); or

Inner life (activity of the mind or of the soul).

Each of these uses has shades of meaning. Each focuses on a different aspect of the person: body, mind, spirit, will, soul, social interaction. But they are overlapping categories, true layers of meaning and inference that are almost never used exclusively. When we talk about life, we are usually talking about some *combination* of the qualities and activities listed above.

Given all that complexity, is there anything we can say is *the* meaning of *life?* We might propose an incomplete definition:

Definition

The terms *life* or *alive* refer to the qualities of awareness and comprehension, and the capacities for activity and response, within a range determined by their context. All life is self-initiating, self-directing, self-sustaining activity and power.

The life of the human being is one of relating to others.

Quotes demonstrating the layers of use and meaning

1. Life, as in being alive (and not dead)

"When we pass through the stage normally called 'death we will not lose anything but the limitations and powers that specifically correspond to our present mastery over our body, and to our availability and vulnerability to and through it. We will no longer be able to act and be acted on by means of it." (DC 394)

2. Life, as a kind of understanding and response-ability (as in what choices and ideas are "living" and accessible)

"[A] cabbage has certain powers of action and response and a corresponding level of life …. But a live cabbage can make no response to, say, a ball of string. That is precisely because of the *kind* of life that is in it. Though alive as a cabbage, it is *dead* to the realm of play … A live cabbage, though dead to one realm (that of play) is yet alive in another—that of the soil, the sun and the rain." (HG 148)

"Human beings were once alive to God. They were created to be responsive to and interactive with him. Adam and Eve lived in a conversational relationship with their Creator, daily renewed. When they mistrusted God and disobeyed him, that cut them off from the realm of the Spirit. Thus they became dead in relation to it—much as a kitten is dead to arithmetic. God had said of the forbidden tree, 'in the day you eat of it you shall die' (Gen 2:17). And they did …. Biologically they continued to live, of course. But they ceased to be

178

responsive and interactive in relation to God's cosmic rule in his kingdom." (HG 148)

3.   Life in the spirit, life from above, and life under the reign of God

"It would be necessary for God to confer an additional level of life on them and their children, through 'being born from above,' (Jn 3:3) in order for them once again to be alive to God, to be able to respond toward him and to act within the realm of the Spirit … . This is not merely to be born again in the sense of *repeating* something or to make a new start from the same place. Instead it is a matter of an *additional* kind of birth whereby we become aware of and enter into the spiritual kingdom of God …. Those born of the Spirit manifest a different kind of life. Remember that a life is a *definite range of activities and responses.* The spiritually born exhibit a life deriving from an invisible spiritual realm and its power." (HG 148-51)

4.   Life, as in daily activity (what we do with our days)

"(When I speak of real life in this book, I always mean the totality of the events we are actually involved in and the actions we actually carry out.)" (RH 94)

5.   Inner life (activity of the mind, heart, or soul)

"[Spiritual] formation may be thought of as the shaping of the inner life, the spirit, or the spiritual side of the human being. The formation of the heart or will (which I believe is best taken as the spirit) of the individual, along with the emotions and intellect, is therefore the primary focus … " (GO 71)

Other relevant citations

DC 86: How should we take care … learning from him …

DC 86-87: Consciousness continues … a richness of experience we have never known before.

DC 206: … our heart is our will, or our spirit … the entire personality.

DC 291: [The] disciple or apprentice of Jesus ... progressively arranging and rearranging their affairs—to do this.

GO 17: In the biblical picture ... live by a power beyond ourselves.

RH 65: Their life will be ... only true human freedom.

RH 163: But of course "the life I now live ... " ... body I now have.

RH 163: Our body is not just ... presence of Christ.

RH 194: Our life in him is whole ... secures everything else.

SD 55: [W]e must look more deeply into the nature of *life* ... infinite resources of God.

SD 115: Even if [we who have the new life from above] waver ... a new force within us that gives us choice.

LOVE

Introduction

"Love is patient. Love is kind …. " (1 Cor. 13) Paul's words have graced many weddings. Maybe too many, since they are so often treated as an admonition about behavior, or a description of proper marital love. In these cases love seems like a strategy, or perhaps a function of will. Or, worst of all, a warm and cozy feeling.

Love is none of these things. It is not a feeling, though affection is. Love is not the product of the will's power. Love is not a strategy for success. Love has the characteristics Paul describes—patience, kindness, joy in the truth, absence of envy—because love is from God, and God has these characteristics. Love is a quality of a Christlike character formed in us as we are re-formed in Christ. It is God's love that redeems the lost and mends the broken; it is our secure knowledge of God's love that allows us to do the same.

The definition of love is simple, but the characteristics, value, and power of love are rich and complex. It is a decent life's work just to describe them well; it is an eternal life's effort to display them.

Definition

Love is the will to good. Encouragement and actions on behalf of a person's good are love, and give life. One who loves promotes the good, or wills the benefit and strength, of the beloved; this is the nature of God. God's love—God's wild and constant willing of our good—and our trusting knowledge of it enables our own love of others.

181

Quotes

1.   Love is the will to good.

"First, what exactly is love? It is will to good or 'bene-volence.' We love something or someone when we promote its good for its own sake." (RH 130)

"Love is not the same thing as desire, for I may desire something without even wishing it well, much less willing its good. I might desire a chocolate ice cream cone, for example. But I do not wish it well; I wish to eat it." (RH 131)

"Love is an overall condition of the embodied, social self poised to promote the goods of human life that are within its range of influence." (*Getting Love Right*)

2.   Encouragement and actions on behalf of a person's good are love, and give life.

"When Jesus speaks of love as the principle of life as it ought to be, he is referring mainly to the posture of *benefiting others in the ordinary relations of ordinary life.*" (KCT 88)

"There is a natural connection and a certain priority to be observed between justice and love. Justice without love will *always* fall short of what needs to be done. It will never be as good as it should be. Justice without love will never do justice to justice, nor will 'love' without justice ever do justice to love. Indeed, it will not be love at all; for *love wills the good of what is loved,* and that must include justice where justice is lacking." (KCT 83)

3.   Love is in the nature of God.

"[God] is Love and sustains his love for us from his basic reality as Love, which dictates his Trinitarian nature. God is in himself a sweet society of love, with a first, second, and third person to complete a social matrix where not only is there love and being loved, but also shared love for another, the third person. Community is formed not by mere love and requited love, which by itself is exclusive, but by shared love for another, which is inclusive." (RH 184)

"It is not hard for God to love, but it is impossible, given his nature, for him not to love." (RH 131)

4.   God's love is what enables ours, through four movements of redemptive love.

"This is the first 'move' of love … 'He first loved us' (1 John 4: 19) …. All other loves are to be measured by this standard (Acts 17: 31).

When we receive what is thus clearly given, the revelation of God's love in Christ, that in turn makes it possible for us to love. Love is awakened in us by him. We feel its call— and first to love Jesus himself, and then God. … This is the second movement in the return to love: 'We love, because He first loved us.'

But the second movement is inseparable from the third movement: our love of others who love God …. love of neighbor as oneself.

And loving others under God will ensure that we are loved by others. For to the others in our community of love, we are the 'other whom they love because they love and are loved by God. The fellowship of Christ's apprentices in kingdom living is a community of love (John 13: 34-35). This is the fourth movement in the process of redeeming love.

Here, then, is the full account of the movements of love in our lives: We are loved by God who is love, and in turn we love him, and others through him, who in turn love us through him. Thus is love made perfect or complete." (RH 132)

Other relevant citations

DC11: God's desire for us … totally competent love.

DC 22: He intended to be … in practical terms.

DC 64: So we must understand … but indispensable old word *love.*

DC 130: [Jesus'] overall picture … the one in the heavens, is perfect and whole.

KCT 155: We know that the nature of this life is love …. precisely God in action that we are experiencing.

RH 131: In such a world God intrudes … and pays the price for it.

RH 183: To merely welcome another … drawing on the abundance of God

RH 183: Love is not a feeling … world for good.

SD 157-59: When we gather "in the name" of Jesus … Church is for catching it and practicing it …

MARRIAGE (AND DIVORCE)

Introduction

Marriage is the central relationship of Christian community. It's not because of the stability implied by marriage. Nor is marriage either proof of or prop for "family values." Marriage is central because it is the mutual submission of two persons into a unity through love.

Love and, because of love, mutual submission together are the form of Christian community. Love and mutual submission is what unity and community in Christ *mean*: agape fellowship. The unity of marriage is an instance of the unity among people in Christ, rather than an independently holy form of relationship.

Added to marriage is the peculiar intimacy borne of sexuality and constant contact, making it a powerful instrument in the development of holiness.

All this is why divorce is so devastating, and why Jesus thought to discuss it. Divorce is the severing of a singular unity and a breach of mutual submission. It is the painful proof of the loss of agape fellowship. It is not a crime, and may be for the best, but it is always a tragedy.

Definition

Marriage is the relationship and activity of two people in constant mutual submission—the laying down of one's life— under the law of love, in the most intimate and encompassing of human relationships. Marriage includes sexuality and may include romance or attraction, but these are neither purpose nor catalyst nor sustaining element of the union. Marriage is a fundamental aspect of Christian community and of social relations.

Quotes

1.   Marriage is the relationship and activity of two people in constant mutual submission—the laying down of one's life—under the law of love, in the most intimate and encompassing of human relationships.

"Disciples must, above all, be convinced and must convince their children that people cannot build a marriage upon either sexual attraction or romantic love alone and that the goodness which is in these is available only within properly agapized homes and communities. The basis of the Christly marriage and family is mutual subordination to the good of others out of a respect for Christ …. The basis for divorce among disciples is precisely the same as the basis for marriage. Where it is the case that the persons involved in a marriage would be substantially better off if the marriage were dissolved, the law of love dictates that a divorce should occur. If indeed the divorce is realized as a consequent of the law of love, the evil which is present in most divorces will not be present—and, indeed, very few divorces will occur. But the disciple will make sure of his or her obedience to the law of love in any divorce by making God his lawyer and judge through prayer." (*Marriage and Divorce*)

2.   Marriage includes sexuality and may include romance or attraction, but these are neither purpose nor catalyst nor sustaining element of the union.

"[The biblical view of the rightness of sex, generally] is tied instead to a solemn and public covenant for life between two individuals, and sexual arousal and delight is a response to the gift of a uniquely personal intimacy with the whole person that each partner has conferred in enduring faithfulness upon the other." (DC 163)

"[The basis for marriage] takes into account such matters as sexual gratification (I Cor. 7) and romantic love, both of which are God's creations and limited goods. But neither sex nor romance is to serve as the basis of marriage among the disciples. Either may serve as one and perhaps a final consideration in the decision to marry or not

186

… but neither is to be regarded as the reason why X and Y should get and stay married. The New Testament regards romantic love as such a negligible factor in marriage that it does not even mention it." (*Marriage and Divorce*)

3.   Marriage is a fundamental aspect of Christian community and of social relations.

"To heal the open sore of social existence, there is no doubt we must start with the marriage relationship-or, more inclusively, with how men and women are together in our world. If that relationship is wrong in its many dimensions, all who come through it will be seriously damaged … Consequently, spiritual formation, and all our efforts as Christians to minister to people, must focus on this humanly most central relationship." (RH 193)

Other relevant citations

DC 169: The intent in marriage … no matter how much *worse* it would have been for them to stay together.

RH 190: The problem is … a religious ceremony.

RH 190: [Marriage is] the kind of constant … one whole person.

RH 191: The "mutual submission to each other in awe of the Lord," … one part to a larger part of the same home.

RH 191: To be married is to give oneself … of his or her being.

RH 191: [Marriage includes] constant sacrificial submission … what marriage involves.

SD 170-171: In sexuality the intermingling of persons … It is a contradiction of terms …

Exercise—Forms of marriage

One of the great debates in our time is about gay marriage: the marriage of two people of the same sex. The premises of the debate range from a concern for social justice and legal equality (pro), to Adam and Eve as the archetype for marriage (con), to society's interest in stable families (pro or con, depending). Most of the arguments have been heard so often that they are worn out, often providing plenty of heat but precious little light.

If you are interested in this debate, you might try sitting with the definition proposed here. Does it provide you any new insights? Does it give cool light, illuminating but not inflaming the topic? How might this understanding of marriage provide guidance for legal policy? Church policy? Personal morality?

MIND

Introduction

"The primary freedom we have is always the choice of where we will place our minds." (GO 54) That is a good thing, because in the battle for sanity, sanctity, health, and wholeness our minds are our most powerful allies. They are also our most treacherous enemies. Though we like to blame the serpent, Adam and Eve's minds caused the Fall (Gen. 3); yet David's composed the Psalms. Our minds control what our bodies reach for and largely determine whether our heart is on board or not.

The apostle Paul wrote, "Do not be conformed to this world, but be transformed by the renewing of your minds" (Rom. 12:2). Our minds aren't everything, but of the five aspects of the human self (mind, body, heart, soul, social), they need our greatest attention and effort.

Definition

The mind is the aspect of the human person that contains, controls, and creates thoughts and feelings, which are distinguishable though inseparable. The thoughts and feelings we have and the visions they create shape every desire, choice, and intention. As a result, what one allows one's mind to dwell on largely determines how one understands and reacts to the world. To be formed into Christlikeness requires replacing "worldly" objects of the mind with good ones—those of Jesus himself. Nonetheless, re-formation of the soul requires not only the renewing of the mind but also the actions of the body and the choices of the will, all of which are interconnected.

Quotes

1.   The mind is the aspect of the human person that contains, controls, and creates thoughts and feelings, which are distinguishable though inseparable.

"Thought is a subdimension of the mind." (GO 57)

"What is thinking? It is the activity of searching out what must be true, or cannot be true, in the light of given facts or assumptions. It extends the information we have and enables us to see the 'larger picture'—to see it clearly and to see it wholly. And it undermines false or misleading ideas and images as well. It reveals their falseness to those who wish to know." (RH 104)

2.   The thoughts and feelings we have and the visions they create, shape every desire, choice, and intention. What one allows one's mind to dwell on largely determines how one understands and reacts to the world.

"Images, in particular, are motivational far beyond our conscious mind, and they are not under rational control. We must take care that we are nourished constantly on good and godly ones, without necessarily being able to see and say what is wrong with the others." (RH 111)

"Confusion is the enemy of spiritual orientation." (RH 175)

"If we allow everything access to our mind, we are simply asking to be kept in a state of mental turmoil or bondage. For nothing enters the mind without having an effect for good or evil." (RH 111)

3.   To be formed into Christlikeness requires replacing "worldly" objects of the mind with good ones—those of Jesus himself.

"It is through the action of the word of God upon us, throughout us and with us that we come to have the mind of Christ and thus to live fully in the kingdom of God." (HG 148)

"The process of spiritual formation in Christ is one of progressively replacing those destructive images and ideas with the images and ideas that filled the mind of Jesus himself." (RH 102)

" [One main part of formation], and by far the most fundamental, is to *form the insights and habits of the student's mind so that it stays directed toward God.* When this is adequately done, a full heart of love will go out toward God, and joy and obedience will flood the life." (DC 325)

4.   Nonetheless, re-formation of the soul requires not only the renewing of the mind but also the actions of the body, and the choices of the will, all of which are interconnected.

"What we think is, in the adult person, very much a matter of what we allow ourselves to think, and what we feel is very much a matter of what we allow ourselves to feel. Moreover, what we think is very much a matter of what we wish and seek to think, and what we feel is very much a matter of what we wish and seek to feel. In short, the condition of our mind is very much a matter of the direction in which our will is set." (RH 141-42)

"Our mind on its own is an extremely feeble instrument, whose power over life we constantly tend to exaggerate. We are incarnate beings in our very nature, and we live from our bodies. If we are to be transformed, the body must be transformed, and that is not accomplished by talking about it." (DC 322)

Other relevant citations

GO 58: We have to think ... Here is our action.

RH 34: [Just] as thought and feeling are inseparable, so volition ... both thought and feeling.

RH 38: Thus there is more to the mind than ... though mind intermingles with body, and so on.

RH 98: Christian spiritual formation is ... a culture of the kingdom of God.

RH 99: Ideas and images … even blind us to what lies plainly before us.

RH 99-100: Ideas and images are … our idea of God and the associated images.

RH 104: We must seek the Lord … his thought life will possess us.

RH 106: To bring the mind to dwell … be before our minds.

RH 110: [If] we are to use our minds … constant openness and learning.

RH 114: [If] we take in God through his Word … God will see to it!

RH 141: The will is totally dependent … in terms of thoughts and feelings.

MORALITY (MORAL RULES AND DECISIONS)

Introduction

True morality is founded in human love, which is derived from divine love. This is, of course, why the "great commandment" is so great: it directly addresses the fundamental requirements of human relationship, which (unsurprisingly) correspond to the law and will of the loving God: Love the Lord your God with all your heart, soul, mind, and strength, and your neighbor as yourself. Living in love, which places one's actions under the law and will of the loving God, guarantees a moral existence. It also is the very definition of living in the kingdom of God.

The contemporary challenge to morality is what Dallas referred to as the elimination of moral knowledge from the knowledge institutions of our society. There are reasons for this, but the effective outcome is that:

Moral standards have come to be regarded as mere displays of social and economic power, and those who employ them as blind or hypocritical;

People have the idea that morality is actually harmful to any prospect of a full and free life;

What we call knowledge of non-material reality (excepting the "pure" sciences) is really opinion; and

What we now call "freedom" is simply the permission to enjoy pleasure.

Definition

Morality is the standard that tells us how to will the good of others—that is, how to love. Moral rules provide the one who loves with guidance for social interaction.

Quotes

1.   Morality is the standard that tells us how to will the good of others—that is, how to love.

"[Jesus'] overall picture of moral fulfillment and beauty in the kingdom of the heavens ... is one of heartfelt love toward all, including those who would be happy if we dropped dead. This love does not consist of acts and projects but is a pervasive condition of vision, joy, and love in which we habitually reside. It is a love of the same quality as God's love. We are to be 'perfect' or whole *as* our Father, the one in the heavens, is perfect and whole." (DC 130)

2.   Moral rules provide the one who loves with guidance for social interaction.

"Moral rules are subordinate to the moral attitude or disposition of love ... . law is not sufficient for love ... You can keep the law as divinely formulated *without* loving your neighbor or even yourself." (KCT 90)

"[Moral] rights depend, for their effective implementation, upon a certain condition in human community. If the community is not one of a high level of moral substance (that is, not predominantly one of morally good people, both in official positions and throughout the population), then moral rights will, at best, degenerate into mere legal rights; and even then they will be continually subject to failure in the context of need, because the individuals involved in such contexts do not act to support them. Those legal rights—where they exist—will also be, at most, honored in the letter, and not in the spirit of human dignity, as Kant and those of similar moral outlook would understand human dignity." (*Moral Rights, Moral Responsibility, and the Contemporary Failure of Moral Knowledge*)

Other relevant citations

HG 106-07: "If our lives conform to the general counsels of God for his people as given to us in the written Word as a whole, then we are perfectly within God's general as well as moral will."

RH 183: This "relating" quality … is the basic reality of a moral existence…

DC 181: [W]hat action we *are* to take … to sacrifice what we simply want.

Exercise—Morality, character, law, and love

Many of us adults have a preschooler's grip on morality: we are mostly self-centered but know that there are rules, some of which we follow when it is convenient. As adults we try to justify the rules that we mostly obey and deflate the ones we flout. We know that morality and character are connected, and that love is somehow involved in law, but left to our own devices morality is about the other guy's getting justice while we get grace. At our best, we know that God has a lot to do with it, and that God's love energizes all of it.

Set aside for a while the idea that your moral rules are the right ones. Now imagine someone who is truly moral—not successful or rich or savvy or a shemozzle. Sit with your image of your Really Moral Person, and ask: Is this person someone whose rules guide behavior, or someone whose behavior seems to just spring from inside? What is the relationship between moral activity and character? Between obeying the law and living in love?

Jot down your answers, then read the entries for *character, law, love, and morality.* How does your Really Moral Person look now?

Finally, write down the characteristics and general activities of your Really Moral person. Would you be able to be their friend? Would you want to do so?

MORALLY GOOD PERSON

Introduction

The concept of the morally good person is explicitly discussed in a number of Dallas' articles, and implicitly in his work on moral knowledge, character development, and "the four great questions of life." Notice that moral goodness is based on quality of character and intention, rather than on activity or belief system. It is the will of the morally good person that allows for right action to emanate from good character.

Definition

A morally good person is one whose character is good, and whose will is set on bringing about what is good.

Quotes

"The morally good person is a person who is devoted to advancing the various goods of human life with which they are effectively in contact, in a manner that respects their relative degrees of importance and the extent to which the actions of the person in question can actually promote the existence and maintenance of those goods. Thus, moral goodness is a matter of the organization of the human will called 'character'." (Why It Matters If You Are Moral)

"The morally good person is, I suggest, to be thought of as one who is admired and imitated just for what he or she is, and without any essential reference to specific relationships, talents, skills or useful traits they may have." (*Faith, Hope and Love as the Indispensable Foundations of Moral Realization*)

PEACE

Introduction

As one of the three main elements of the fruit of the Spirit, peace is almost always associated with love and joy in Dallas' work. Though peace is associated with an absence of conflict, it is not an absence at all. Rather, peace is the presence of security and hope. Peace is what allows a disciple to remain consistently unruffled by outside turmoil or critique. When you are at peace, you feel secure in God's good world.

Peace is what disciples get from a life shot throughout by justified faith in God's love, grace, goodness and power. It is the result of abandonment to God, when your will is truly surrendered to God. Peace is constituted by the deep rest that comes from knowing and understanding that you are perfectly safe in God's great universe, because God is in charge.

Definition

Peace is the deep rest and assurance of good that comes from complete abandonment to God.

Quotes

"With this magnificent God positioned among us, Jesus brings the assurance that our universe is a *perfectly safe place for us to be.*" (DC 66)

"The secret to this peace is, as great apprentices of Jesus have long known, being abandoned to God …. the person who is heartily abandoned to God knows that all shall be well because God is in charge of his or her life." (RH 135)

"Peace is the rest of will that results from assurance about 'how things will turn out.' It is always a form of active engagement with good, plus assurance that things will turn out well." (RH 133)

Other relevant citations

RH 209: Rest to our soul is … child with its mother.

GO 212: [The children of God] have learned … love, joy, and peace.

DC 400: [The] kingdom come … limitless goodness and greatness of the triune personality of God, its source.

SD 263: Nondiscipleship costs abiding peace … that abundance of life Jesus said he came to bring.

Example—Psalm 131

One of Dallas' favorite examples of peace was Jesus' sleeping on the storm-tossed boat in Luke 8. Jesus slept because he lay in his Abba's arms in perfect trust. Another outstanding example of the peace that comes from abandonment to God is found in Psalm 131. As you meditatively read the Psalm, pay attention to the language of the weaned child: the image should be of an infant who is completely satisfied, has finished suckling at its mother's breast, and lies content and safe.

My heart is not proud, Lord, my eyes are not haughty;
I do not concern myself with great matters or things too wonderful for me.
But I have calmed and quieted myself, I am like a weaned child with its mother; like a weaned child I am content.

Israel, put your hope in the Lord both now and forevermore. (NIV)

PERSON

Introduction

In normal conversation we tend to associate persons with their bodies. If you were at a party, and, having noticed someone you know named Kwame, said, "Oh, there is Kwame over near the table," you would likely be surprised to discover that the person of Kwame was dwelling in another body, or floating around the room. Kwame might be surprised too.

To be a person is not necessarily to have a body, or even to be a human being. Spiritual beings, such as God and the angels, are persons. To be a person is to have a certain *kind* of life, one that involves consciousness and will and dignity. In human beings, that includes having a body.

Dallas uses the word *person* in both senses, but even in the more casual manner — using *person* to indicate human beings — it is the *kind* of life that makes the human being a person.

> ## Definition
>
> A person is a living being that has a certain kind of life. Persons have souls, spirits (or "wills" or "hearts") and minds and are able to exercise self-determination and dominion. Thus persons are entities who are capable of having a kingdom.

Quotes

1. A person is a living being that has a certain kind of life.

"A person is a living entity that has a certain kind of life: primarily one of self-determination in terms of adopted values, with the possibility (and vital need) of worship." (GO 139)

"[In 'death'] the body as intermediary between the person and the physical world is losing its function as the soul prepares for a new arrangement ... The life we now have as the persons we now are will continue, and continue in the universe in which we now exist. Our experience will be much clearer, richer, and deeper, of course, because it will be unrestrained by the limitations now imposed upon us by our dependence upon our body." (DC 393-94)

2.   Persons have souls, spirits, and minds and are able to exercise self-determination and dominion.

"With the soul, everything else comes along. But still, the person is not identical with his soul. There is much to the person other than the soul, and in this lies hope for the restructuring of the broken and corrupted soul." (GO 146)

"Any being that has say over nothing at all is no person ... Such 'persons' would not even be able to command their own body or their own thoughts." (DC 22)

"Why should self-determination be regarded as valuable? Because that is your humanity, your 'personhood,' and it is of greater value and 'meaningfulness' than pleasure, power and survival. Its loss brings loss of meaning, no 'carry over,' no transitiveness, no life energy." (*Professions and the Public Interest in Human Life*)

3.   Thus, persons are entities able to have a kingdom.

"Every last one of us has a 'kingdom' ... a realm that is uniquely our own, where our choice determines what happens. Here is a truth that reaches into the deepest party of what it is to be a person." (DC 21)

Other relevant citations

DC 21: In creating human beings ... they be persons.

DC 25-26: The person of God himself ... is *within* his kingdom.

DC 77: Persons rarely ... wanted.

GO 104: Within the invisible dimension ... lies the human spirit.

RH 19: We each become ... type of character.

SD 7: These responses ... the kind of righteousness that God himself has.

SD 76: There is an essential continuity … his or her body

Example—Chickens from outer space

To teach the concept of personhood, philosophy teachers have long used the following thought experiment. Suppose you travel to another planet and discover that nearly everything is the same as it is on Earth. This planet has roughly the same atmosphere, creatures, ecosystems, technological abilities as your own. On this planet are creatures that look like humans, but scratch at the ground, peck at bugs, crow and cluck, and use no tools. There are also creatures that look like chickens, but they speak clearly defined languages, use tools, gather for events, nurture their young, and organize themselves to achieve greater aims. When you call back to Earth with your findings, which creatures do you call the "people" of the planet?

In May 2013, India's Ministry of Environment and Forests issued a statement banning the use of dolphins in captivity for entertainment purposes. The statement read, in part: "Whereas cetaceans in general are highly intelligent and sensitive, and various scientists who have researched dolphin behavior have suggested that the unusually high intelligence; as compared to other animals means that dolphin should be seen as "non-human persons" and as such should have their own specific rights and is morally unacceptable to keep them captive for entertainment purpose,". India's focus on dolphins' intelligence and sensitivity is different from Dallas' concern for self-determination and the need of worship, but what might it mean for the chickens from outer space in the example above?

POWER

Introduction

The definition of power is simple and straightforward: the capacity to accomplish an end. God has power. An electric drill has power. A crying baby has extraordinary power. While the definition of power is simple, its characteristics and manifestations, however, are many and diverse. For example:

Power is related to physical energy;

Power may be embodied (reside in physical objects or persons) or not;

Power may be personal (residing in persons) or not;

Power may be shared between God and humans. Some examples include grace (God's empowering activity), reigning over our kingdoms (and his), and the new life that comes with regeneration (which is power to become the obedient children of God).

Dallas used *power* to encompass all these attendant attributes, so don't be surprised if all of them come up in your reading of a passage. The one thing they have in common? That power effects ends.

Definition

Power is the capacity to accomplish an end.

Quotes

1. Power is related to physical energy

" 'Power' has its tie to mass and energy, for God and for us. This is a physical concept, not a psychological or analogical one. God's power is the ultimate extreme of E (qua e=mc^2)" (SD 53-55)

"We know that this 'source' [of the physical world] must be of great power to have produced the physical universe … If we are to take seriously the equation e=mc^2, the source of the physical world must involved enough e (energy) to translate into the m (mass) of the physical universe. That's a lot of energy." (KCT 110)

2.   Power may be embodied.

"[The] body is the place of our direct power. It is the little 'power pack'." (GO 89)

"Electricity, magnetism, and gravity, by contrast are embodied nonpersonal powers." (SD 64)

3.   Power may be unembodied.

"[Spirit] is unembodied personal power. Ultimately it is God, who *is* spirit." (SD 64)

"God who is, paradigmatically, unbodily personal power." (GO 48)

4.   Power may be shared between God and humans

a. Human power

"Now, a discipline is an activity in our power, which we pursue in order to become able to do what we cannot do by direct effort." (GO 86)

"Human beings have only some small element of spirit—unbodily, personal power--right at the center of who they are and who they become." (RH 33-34)

b. Power of humans interacting with God (in the Kingdom of God)

"I believe men and women were designed by God, in the very constitution of their human personalities, to carry out his rule by meshing the relatively little power resident in their own bodies with the power inherent in the infinite Rule or Kingdom of God … . Their rule was indeed their rule—their understanding, their desire, their choice— but it was exercised by means of a power greater than their own bodies could muster, a power conveyed through a personal relation with the Creator of all things." (SD 54)

"[Faith] is in its very nature a power and a life … a powerful life force …

1. The presence of a new power *within* the individual, erupting into a break with the past through turning in repentance and the release of forgiveness ….

2. An immediate but also a developing transformation of the individual character and personality ….

3. A significant, extrahuman power over the evils of this present age and world, exercised both by individuals and by the collective church" (SD 40)

"Prayer is God's arrangement for a safe *power sharing* with us in his intention to bless the world through us. In response to prayer we see good accomplished far beyond what we are capable of and in a form suited to the wisdom of God—not just to what we think we know about the situation we are praying for." (KCT 160)

"[Only] constant students of Jesus will be given adequate power to fulfill their calling to be God's person for their time and their place in this world. They are the only ones who develop the character which makes it safe to have such power." (GO 17)

c. Power associated with regeneration—the "new life" of Christ residing within one, or with grace.

"Life is everywhere inseparable from power, and new life means new powers. This power is, in the New Testament conception, *literally* located in the body of the redeemed or spiritually enlivened person. [See the power expenditure of Jesus in Mark 5:25-30.] … . [W]e are here dealing with a new kind of life, and that to deny the powers associated with it is really to deny the life. [There is no] new life in Christ *without* novel manifestations of power." (SD 122)

Other relevant citations

DC 369: Yet it is God's intent … to his great joy and relief, no doubt.

GO 16: [For] the one who makes sure … looking for people he can trust with his power.

GO 17: [On] the biblical picture … live by a power beyond ourselves.

GO 51: Christian spirituality is supernatural … a "life from above."

GO 47: [In] Romans 8:1–14 you find … visible as well as triumphant.

SD 61-62: The astonishing human power to *use* … are yet to be fully known.

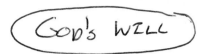

THE RANGE OF GOD'S EFFECTIVE WILL

Introduction

The phrase *range of effective will* is used to define the *kingdom* or *reign* of a person. Simply put, the range of your effective will is limited to the circumstances under which what you say goes, or where your will is done. In the case of humans, the range of one's effective will is limited by one's power and influence. In the case of God, the range of effective will is unlimited, except for the fact that God has granted effective will to both human and spiritual beings. In effect, God has limited the efficacy of God's own will. Therefore, while God could have his will done everywhere and in every circumstance, God has chosen to live *in relationship* with human and spiritual persons: beings who may also exercise their wills.

Definition

The range of God's effective will is wherever what God wants done, is done.

Quotes

"God's own 'kingdom,' or 'rule,' is the range of his effective will, where what he wants done is done. The person of God himself and the action of his will are the organizing principles of his kingdom, but everything that obeys those principles, whether by nature or by choice, is *within* his kingdom … . [The] social and political realm, along with the individual heart, is the only place in all of creation where the kingdom of God, or his effective will, is currently permitted to be absent … ." (DC 25)

"The kingdom of God is the range of God's effective will, where what God wants done is done. It is, like God himself, from everlasting to everlasting … The planet Earth and its immediate surroundings seem to be the only place in creation where God permits his will to be not done." (RH 86)

"To [Jesus'] eyes this is a God-bathed and God-permeated world. It is a world filled with a glorious reality, where every component is within the range of God's direct knowledge and control—though he obviously permits some of it, for good reasons, to be for a while otherwise than as he wishes." (DC 61-62)

Example—Bad things happen

A terrible truth of human existence is that bad things happen to people who don't deserve them. We might not be upset if a mass murderer got hit by a drunk driver, but we would be stricken if it happened to a child. Even those with no connection to the child, who are not grieving the loss, would shake their heads in disbelief or anger. Someone would ask: if God loved that child, why didn't he prevent this?

There may be no totally satisfactory answer to that question, since God's deep motivations are a mystery. But it is true that for human beings to have free will and make tragic errors in judgment, God must refrain from having perfectly effective will. We must experience the consequences of our choices in order to *be* persons, that is, creatures who can and do exercise our wills, as they are influenced by our bodies, minds, circumstances and spirits.

Dallas argued that we do not have free will, actually, so long as we are not free to consistently choose the good. As long as our habits, pride, and selfishness restrict or direct our wills, we are not free, and our habits, pride, and selfishness will cause bad things to happen.

210

REALITY

Introduction

That old "can't see the forest for the trees" saying applies to the concept of reality. Most of the philosophical work of the last hundred years or so has been questioning whether perception of any kind can be trusted, especially to discern something that could be properly termed reality. Go too deeply on this one and you will start to wonder whether you have been reading this book at all, or if there is a substantial "this" to be read! But Dallas was a philosophical realist: he believed there is a *there* there beyond anyone's perceptions. So if you are actually reading, then you are reading some*thing.*

To get a handle on the scope of reality, begin by assuming that everything accessible by the five senses is real. You might have sensed them poorly or drawn bad inferences from your sensing, but the accessible object is real. Add the idea that the equations and concepts of pure science (such as math) are true, if not materially "real." That much will get you to the most limited secular notion of reality.

Now add the idea that everything accessible accurately through experience is also real, whether it is sensible or not. Also add the idea that their correspondence to reality is what makes the statements of authorities credible; now you can accept the reality described by credible authorities. These two ideas will help you get at feelings, thoughts, non-material persons and objects, and personally unobserved objects and phenomena.

Reality, then, would include both material and non-material objects, persons, states, feelings, and conditions that are accessible through experience, sensation, or logic. This would include things like God, the Trinitarian community, moral truths, and love.

Another way to put it: whatever is the object of knowledge is real.

But the third definition (a classic Dallas quip) listed below probably sums it up best.

Definition

Reality includes both material and non-material objects, persons, states, feelings, and conditions that are accessible through accurate experience, sensation, or logic.

Whatever is the object of knowledge is real.

Reality is what you run into when you're wrong.

Quotes

1.   Reality includes both material and non-material objects, persons, states, feelings, and conditions that are accessible through accurate experience, sensation, or logic.

"[The] ultimate reality … is God and his kingdom." (DC 353)

"God is spirit and exists at the level of reality where the human heart, or spirit, also exists, serving as the foundation and source of our visible life." (DC 194)

" '[Baptizing disciples] in the name' refers to surrounding them, immersing them in the reality of the Trinitarian community." (GO 44)

"[Not] all of reality involves space … Our faith may all too easily fall victim to our mind's tendency to spacialize everything … . There is no reason in the established truths of science to suppose that God cannot reach us and be with us in order to guide and communicate with us. There is plenty of room left for God in the picture of the world presented to us by contemporary science … . the whole of reality is something penetrated by God." (HG 74-78)

"The greatest of divides between human beings and human cultures is between those who regard the visible world as being of primary importance—possibly alone real or at least the touchstone of reality—and those who do not." (HG 219)

2.   Whatever is the object of knowledge is real.

212

"All these things show Jesus' cognitive and practical mastery of every phase of reality: physical, moral, and spiritual … " (DC 95)

"All religions purport to explain what is real and what is right. That is reality, and, if correct, is knowledge." (KCT 21-24)

"Those who operate on the wrong information are likely never to know the reality of God's presence in the decisions which shape their lives and will miss the constant divine companionship for which their souls were made." (HG 10)

"People perish for lack of knowledge, because *only knowledge permits assured access to reality*, and reality does not adjust itself to accommodate our false beliefs, errors, or hesitations in action." (KCT 39)

3.   Reality is what you run into when you're wrong.

"[We] can think of reality as what you run into when you are wrong. And if you do, you'll recognize that most of us have some first hand acquaintance with reality and truth, which are so vital and so important for human life that we can't really survive in the academy or elsewhere without them." (*Truth: Can We Do Without It?*)

Other relevant citations

DC 11: God's desire for us … totally competent love.

DC 41: Moment-to-moment human reality … eternal living.

DC 76: God relates to space … in the body of Jesus.

DC 92-94: Quite simply, [Jesus'] work and teaching … They cannot be separated from it … . Our commitment to Jesus … to be competent.

KCT 123: Since there is such a vast nonphysical (spiritual) reality … of religion and the Bible.

RH 15: [It] is a bad idea to deny … is one.

RH 17: In its nature the physical … the physical world never can be.

RH 97: [One] commonly identifies … pure and simple.

REDEMPTION

Introduction

Redemption is often used to describe the effect of Jesus' atoning sacrifice on the cross, the idea being that his death bought humans back from or paid the price of sin. Dallas tended to use the word as a marker for one step in the process of salvation, without reference to atonement. Redemption in this sense is a rescue or a retrieval from the power of sin, rather than a ransom paid to escape the consequences of sin.

Definition

Redemption is the second step in salvation: the retrieval of all five aspects of the human person—the person's actual life—from alienation and opposition to God. This is the deliverance from the power of sin. It is a transformative process of divine and human action; as such it is part of sanctification.

Quotes

1.   Redemption is the second step in salvation: the retrieval of all five aspects of the human person—the person's actual life—from alienation and opposition to God. This is the deliverance from the power of sin.

"Redemption in Christ is a retrieving of the entire person from alienation from God and opposition to God." (*Gray Matter and the Soul*)

"In today's presentation of the gospel, Jesus' death is primarily presented as a ransom that deals with guilt and the effects of guilt regarding our standing before God. But there is more to life than guilt. Once you have been forgiven, you still have to live. Jesus is about the redemption of actual life from actual sin. It is by entering into his life, which is still ongoing on earth, that we are delivered from actual sin. The New Testament is absolutely clear on this. You just take Colossians 3, Philippians 3, 1 John and Titus 3. All make it clear that the righteousness which is by faith is a matter of being delivered from the evil that is around us in action and that we are in danger of falling into ourselves." (*Rethinking Evangelism*)

2.   It is a transformative process of divine and human action; as such it is part of sanctification.

"Here we find the positive role of the body in the process of redemption, as we choose those uses of our body that advance the spiritual life." (SD 40)

"Here as in all the other dimensions of our life, the progression of redemption in our relations to others depends upon what we do as well as what God does for us and in us. And in order to do our part in the process of spiritual formation of social relations we must deeply identify and understand what is wrong in our relations with others (whether that wrong is coming from us or toward us) and how it can be changed." (RH 187)

"Of course, we do our righteous deed because of our redemption, not *for* our redemption." (SD 119)

"Human initiative is not canceled by redemption; it is heightened by immersion in the flow of God's life." (HG 208)

Other relevant citations

RH 99: The cross presents ... that brings redemption.

RH 258: [This] has been the understanding ... they aren't separable—ever.

SD 92-93: [The role of disciplines] rests upon the nature ... "quickening spirit."

SD 111: Paul understood redemption ... of the body and the mind.

SD 114-18: [Three] stages of redemption as a real, psychological process.

» Stage 1: Baptized into Christ

» Stage 2: "Reckon"—A New Attitude

» Stage 3: Submitting our members to righteousness

216

Example—A nickel back

In what now seems like the olden days, you could save the glass bottle after you drank your soda and return it to the grocery store. The clerk would give you a nickel back for each bottle you brought it. That nickel wasn't a gift or payment; it was a refund of a deposit you had unwittingly paid when you bought the soda. That deposit was the redemption value of the bottle; when you turned in the bottle you redeemed it—you got it back.

This is closer to Dallas' meaning of redemption. If you are redeemed, it's not because Jesus bought you, or paid a debt that you actually owed. You are redeemed because, like the bottle, you have been returned to where you belong, to the place you can be re-filled.

REGENERATION

Introduction

An oft-forgotten piece of the process of salvation, regeneration occurs along with forgiveness during justification. Regeneration is God's giving of a new life—the *life from above.* It is what enables and kicks off sanctification, which is the transformation of the inner person into Christlikeness. This new kind of life quickens all aspects of the individual, most clearly the soul and spirit (will, heart), and provides the ability to access the power of God and his kingdom, making spiritual re-formation possible.

> ## Definition
> Regeneration is the unique event in a human being's earthly existence in which a new kind of life enters into him or her.

Quotes

"But is there a recognizably Christian view of salvation—one prominent in scripture and history—that does have spiritual formation as a natural part or outgrowth of "salvation," understood to be an identifiable status (sometimes, at least, associated with a specific event)? … it comes in the form of the theological concept of regeneration. This is the event of a new type of life entering into the individual human being. The kind of life that the human being has on its own—its 'natural' life, so to speak—is a kind of 'death' compared to the type of life that begins to move in us at 're-generation.' Once this is mentioned, I believe the person familiar with the New Testament writings will recognize the passage from 'death' to 'life' as a constant biblical theme, where 'life' is a real and powerful presence in the regenerate individual." (*Spiritual Formation as a Natural Part of Salvation*)

"[Spiritual] transformation only happens as each essential dimension of the human being is transformed to Christlikeness under the direction of a regenerate will interacting with constant overtures of grace from God." (RH 41)

Other relevant citations

GO 47: [In] Romans 8:1–14 you find, "All who are led by the Spirit of God are children of God." … visible as well as triumphant.

GO 76: Spiritual formation in Christ … an adequate course of spiritual disciplines.

GO 163: [Conversion to a godly life of faith] involves both reconciliation and regeneration … You are given new life by grace through faith, and in that process, or in the light of it, your sins are, of course, forgiven.

REPENTANCE AND METANOIA

Introduction

The term *repentance* is rarely mentioned in Dallas' books, the Greek word *metanoia* (pronounced *meh-ta-NOY-ah*) even less frequently. His work is largely concerned with the divine-human activity that enables spiritual transformation, and the role of human beings in the kingdom of God. He assumes that "the profound inward turnings of repentance and faith" (DC 343) are prerequisite to formation. He was also aware that its general meaning of "turning around" has been discussed to death.

When Dallas used the word, he meant repentance to be inseparable from our deep sorrow, even horror, over our readiness to do evil and the sin-filled condition of all aspects of our person. Repentance is not an intellectual act, for in the light radiating from the kingdom of God, we see ourselves as we are, and as God sees us. Given that vision of goodness, we cannot help but repent, and long for real change. This longing for real change is called *metanoia*.

To repent is to become aware of God's invitation into the kingdom, recoil with awareness of your sin and brokenness, and rethink your strategy for living, now that the option of the kingdom is at hand.

Definition

Repentance is the inward activity of turning toward God that takes place when we realize the depth and power of our sin-inhabited lives. To repent is to become aware of God's invitation into the kingdom, recoil with awareness of your sin and brokenness, and rethink your strategy for living, now that the option of the kingdom is at hand.

Quotes

"We, then, must change from within. And that is what most of us truly want. The repentance in which we pine for our life and world to really be different, the authentic *metanoia* which Christ opens us to in his gospel … comes upon us as we are given a vision of the majesty, holiness, and goodness of God. It's a vision sufficient to impart a vivid realization of our terrible readiness to mistrust God and hurt others and ourselves as we take things into our own hands. This sharp, heartbreaking realization of *our condition* silences all arguments and hair-splitting rationalization. It makes us simultaneously recoil from God, because we realize that he also sees us for what we are, and yet we reach out for help and refuge in him." (SD 227)

" … the vapid, mass-produced experiences of repentance and faith—if we may indeed call them that—that now are commonly announced as entrance into a new and supernatural life [will not bring us to love and acceptance]." (SD 235)

"In Matthew's account of Jesus' deeds and words, the formulation repeatedly used is the well-known 'Repent, for the kingdom of the heavens is at hand' (3:2; 4:17; 10:7). This is a call for us to reconsider how we have been approaching our life, in light of the fact that we now, in the presence of Jesus, have the option of living within the surrounding movements of God's eternal purposes, of taking our life into his life." (DC 15-16)

RIGHTEOUSNESS AND *DIKAIOSUNE*

Introduction

While not properly a "Willard word," the Greek concept of dikaiosune (pronounced *dee-kai-oh-SOO-nay*) is what Dallas means when he uses the words *righteous* and *righteousness*. In the New Testament, *dikaiosune* refers to the state of character of a really good person, rather than any particular set of actions. Prescribed sets of actions quickly dissolve into legalism, devolving further into self-righteousness. Even if one avoids self-righteousness, one simply cannot expect to consistently perform the right actions Jesus talks about in Matthew 5-7, for example, by force of will and habit. Righteous character—dikaiosune—is required for humble consistency.

Definition

A righteous (or really good) person is one whose character has been transformed into the character (dikaiosune) of the one really good person, that is Christ, and whose actions emanate from that character rather than from adherence to an external standard.

Quotes

"Jesus never expected us simply to turn the other cheek, go the second mile, bless those who persecute us, give unto them that ask, and so forth. These responses, generally and rightly understood to be characteristic of Christlikeness, were set forth by him as illustrative of what might be expected of a new kind of person—one who intelligently and steadfastly seeks, above all else, to live within the rule of God and be possessed by the kind of righteousness that God himself has ... Instead, Jesus did invite people to follow him into that sort of life from which behavior such as loving one's enemies will seem like the only sensible and happy thing to do." (SD 7)

"[In agape love] we achieve living union with, have fully entered into, the kingdom of the heavens. We have sought and found the reigning of God and the kind of dikaiosune he himself has. Out of that union we discover love as a life power that has the marvelous, many-sided expression spelled out by Paul in 1 Corinthians 13 … . it is love that does these things, not us, and that what we are to do is to 'pursue love.' As we 'catch' love, we then find that these things are after all actually being done by us. These things, these godly actions and behaviors, are the result of dwelling in love." (DC 182)

SALVATION

Introduction

Salvation is an essential term in Dallas' work, as it is an essential aspect of the eternal life of the human person. He takes pains to distinguish between a contemporary version of salvation—forgiveness and a ticket to heaven—and a gospel version that is nothing less than new life.

Two ideas are essential to the concept: 1) salvation is a process, not an event or a moment; and 2) life in the kingdom of God is available right now, not merely after bodily death. God partners with an individual who not only accepts God's offer but continues to "work out your salvation with fear and trembling" (Phil. 2:12)

The process of salvation includes repentance and forgiveness (justification), a progressive transformation of the inner person into Christlikeness (sanctification), interactive knowledge and relationship with God (eternal life), and everlasting life after bodily death (glorification). Salvation is initiated and achieved by God's actions of forgiveness (reconciliation), regeneration, redemption, and restoration, all of which are elements of God's saving grace.

Definition

Salvation is not merely forgiveness with a ticket to heaven, but a life lived interactively in the present kingdom of God.

Quotes

"When 'salvation' is spoken of today, where it is spoken of at all, what is almost always meant is entry into heaven when one dies. One is 'saved' if one is now counted by God among those who will be admitted into His presence at death or some point thereafter. This usage of 'salvation' and 'saved' deprives the terminology of the general sense of deliverance." (GO 110)

"He saves us by realistic restoration of our heart to God and then by dwelling there with his Father through the distinctively divine Spirit." (RH 18)

"[The] simple and wholly adequate word for salvation in the New Testament is 'life.'" (SD 37)

"Simple inductive study of the New Testament will, I believe, convince anyone that the primary way of understanding salvation according to it is in terms of a divine life that enters the human being as a gift of God." (*Spiritual Formation as a Natural Part of Salvation*)

"One way I try to express what Salvation is is to say 'It is participating in the life that Jesus is now living on Earth.' … it's participating in the life that Jesus is now living. Christ in me, the hope of Glory." (*Gospel of the Kingdom*)

Other relevant citations

GO 110: [By] no means denying the essential importance of correct belief … entry into heaven as a natural outcome rather than as the central focus.

RH 82: Everyone must be active … is not something we are waiting upon.

SD 28: Why is it that we look upon our salvation as a moment … in our spiritual life.

Example—God is not opposed to effort

If you stay very still and listen closely, you can hear the low rumble of centuries of dearly departed Protestants rolling over in their graves, whispering, "grace, not works! Can't earn God's love!" Okay, maybe it's not that bad, but an opposition between God's grace and our works has made human effort in the process of salvation seem an insult to God. But the idea was never that you shouldn't do anything about your salvation, but that no matter how hard you worked you couldn't earn it or deserve it. Salvation is by grace (God's effort) because your effort could never earn what God offers.

Grace is opposed to earning, not to effort. In fact, God seems to appreciate a little effort; if nothing else it shows that you want to be more like Jesus. If you need proof that salvation might have something to do with effort, scan the Bible for a slacker-hero. Let the rest of us know how you do.

SANCTIFICATION

7

Introduction

Sanctification may be the clearest of six standard theological elements of the process of salvation, the others being justification, reconciliation, regeneration, redemption and glorification. Sanctification is itself a process by which the inner person of an individual comes to resemble Christ's inner person. The end goal of sanctification is Christlikeness. It is, simply put, the process of becoming holy.

The oft-neglected key to sanctification is choice. The disciple must consistently choose to take the actions needed for internal transformation, while depending upon God to do God's part. But God will not do all the heavy lifting; our effort is required. To become like Jesus requires God's justification (repentance, forgiveness, reconciliation), regeneration (the giving of the new life), and ongoing grace, along with our effort.

Sanctification has all but been discarded in the modern Western church, its absence excused by such descriptions as "only human" and "forgiven, not perfect." When Dallas referred to "the great omission" it is sanctification that has been omitted from the gospels of the right and the left, having been replaced by a gospel of sin management limited to justification and behavior.

Definition

Sanctification is the intentional process by which the inner person of an individual comes to resemble that of Christ. It is dependent upon regeneration (the giving of a new life by God), human effort, and God's grace. Sanctification results in an evergrowing and easy obedience to and relationship with God.

229

Quotes

"Sanctification in this life will always be a matter of degree, to be sure, but there is a point in genuine spiritual growth before which the term "sanctification" simply does not apply— just as "hot" when applied to a cup of coffee is a matter of degree, but there is a point before which it is not hot, even if in the process of being heated. … So what shall we say about sanctification in summary? It is a consciously chosen and sustained relationship of interaction between the Lord and his apprentice, in which the apprentice is able to do, and routinely does, what he or she knows to be right before God because all aspects of his or her person have been substantially transformed. Sanctification applies primarily to the moral and religious life, but extends in some measure to the prudential and practical life (acting wisely) as well." (RH 226)

Other relevant citations

RH 224: [Sanctification], as a condition … in the mature children of light.

RH 226: [The] application of redemption is … like Christ in our actual lives.

RH 226: Sanctification is not an experience … the process of spiritual formation.

Example—Restoring a car

Imagine that you have discovered a formerly fine old car available for purchase. Make it a 1931 Duesenberg, or perhaps a 1907 Rolls-Royce: something rare and valuable, possessing the potential for great power and beauty. But it has been neglected and its extraordinary nature is barely discernable. The outside looks mostly okay, but the mechanisms that made it run are shot. The original engine isn't even there. But you see it, you recognize its value, and you pay for it.

You have seen its potential and bought this wreck. Is it now restored? Beautiful? Even functional? Let's say you drop a restored engine in it as soon as you buy it. How is it now? You might be able to use it for something, but it certainly wouldn't be reliable, much less either powerful or street-worthy. Interior and exterior beauty are a long way off; it barely resembles the classic it was designed and made to be. It's going to take work to restore it.

You are not so different from the car. The analogy fails because in the car scenario the owner of the car has to do all the work, which suggests that God takes on the entire process of restoration and formation. But you get the idea: just because you were bought and got a new life-engine doesn't mean the work is finished.

THE SIGNIFICANCE OF A HUMAN LIFE

Introduction

Though he didn't mention it often, the idea that a human life has significance in God's great plan of restoration undergirds both Dallas' understanding of the kingdom and of the purpose of spiritual disciplines. Reigning properly in God's kingdom is the ultimate significance of a human life, thus Jesus' apprentices are "training to reign" in the kingdom of God.

Notice that significance is not about legacy, or the sweet by and by. Remember that God's kingdom is here and now, and that each of us has a kingdom. How we reign over our own kingdom determines how we will reign in God's future kingdom. But even more important: if our kingdom is under the authority of God's kingdom right now, if our will is subordinate to God's, how we reign over our kingdom *is right now* how we are reigning in God's kingdom. Thus the significance of a human life is *not* what it *will do,* but how what you are doing right now influences the right now kingdom of God.

To consistently do right in God's kingdom requires habits of behavior that can only be maintained by a Christlike character. A Christlike character is developed through your effort and God's grace. Hence you are training to reign in God's kingdom. Or you're not. A significant difference and a difference in significance.

Definition

The significance of a human life is found in entering God's kingdom and learning to reign there. Such activity optimally results in a person who may be entrusted by God to do what he or she wants as they reign together over God's kingdom.

Quotes

"The intended significance of the individual life is to enter and to learn God's reign in his kingdom." (DC 250)

"[At the end of the present life] ~~what is of~~ significance is the kind of person one has become." (DC 376)

"Our hunger for significance is a signal of who we are and why we are here, and it also is the basis of humanity's enduring response to Jesus. For he always takes individual human beings as seriously as their shredded dignity demands, and he has the resources to carry through with his high estimate of them." (DC 15)

Example—Taking training and reigning seriously

What are the different parts of your life? Parenting? Being a child or sibling? Driving a taxi? Teaching? Volunteering? Exercising? Cooking? Take a moment to write down the roles you play (e.g. parent), or primary activities (e.g. parenting), in your daily life.

Each of these parts is part of your kingdom. You reign over each area. You may not reign alone, but if you have any say in the outcome you reign. You've probably received some training in each area through watching someone else, taking classes or reading books, or learning through trial and error. Maybe a professional trainer corrected your form at the gym and watched you practice. Maybe your mom showed you how to set the table. Maybe you burned dinner a few times before you got some of the basic techniques right. Instruction plus practice creates training.

What is the common denominator of all these parts? You are, of course. It is you who are all these things or do all these things. And who you are—your inner person—will largely determine how you do what you do. Given that you bring yourself to anything you do, what kind of training do you need in order to bring your best self, your most Christlike self, to every area?

Remember, every area is part of your kingdom: in them you reign. It's your responsibility to reign well, to get the training you need to do so, and to practice seriously so you can and do.

234

SIN

Introduction

Awareness of your own sin can seem like watching the scoreboard at a baseball game: Willpower 2 Sins 37. But counting sins as individual activities or events directs us away from the real problem: sin is a relieveable condition of the body, soul, and will.

As sin is a condition of the person so is it the shape of the current world: we live in a context of sin. This isn't a matter of bad behavior or ugly morals—everyone could be nice to each other and sin would still loom.

It is essentially alienation from God's love, God's interaction, God's law. This alienation makes the things of God seem more distant and less satisfying than the things of the sinful world. To overcome sin's influence we must make choices against the activities of the body and will that reinforce the desires of the mind. We must use our bodies to train the rest of our person to turn toward God, decreasing that alienation.

Those who have received regeneration—an actual new life installed in us—are primed with the possibility of removing sin from our lives. Doing this takes our activity: retraining, not willpower.

[*Definition follows on next page.*]

Definition

Sin is the natural condition of the material world, including material persons, when alienated from God. In persons, sin wounds, corrupts, and breaks the soul.
Sin is not the fleeting or lingering thought about something that turns against God; that is, thoughts are not sins. Thoughts lead through temptation (desire plus inclination) then combine with your willingness to act to make sin. Over time, sin becomes lodged in the habits of the body.
Overcoming sin for the person with the new life is a matter of using your body to retrain the other aspects of your person.

Quotes

1.   Sin is the natural condition of the material world, including material persons, when alienated from God. In persons, sin wounds, corrupts, and deforms the soul

"The condition of normal human life is one where the inner resources of the person are weakened or dead, and where the factors of human life do not interrelate as they were intended by their nature and function to do. This is sin in the singular: not an act but a condition. It is not that we are wrong, but that our inner components are no longer hooked up correctly." (GO 146)

"[Sin] or disobedience to what we know to be right distances us from God and forces us to live on our own. That means it makes soul rest impossible and is very destructive to the soul." (RH 210)

"Sinful practices become their habits, then their choice, and finally their character." (GO 82)

2.   Sin is not the fleeting or lingering thought about something that turns against God; that is, thoughts are not sins. Thoughts lead through temptation (desire plus inclination) then combine with your willingness to act to make sin.

236

"Temptation is the thought plus the inclination to sin--possibly manifested by lingering over the thought or seeking it out." (RH 33)

"Choice is where sin dwells." (RH 46)

3. Over time, sin becomes lodged in the habits of the body.

"[As long] as we are 'at home in the body' (2 Corinthians 5:6), we are still just recovering sinners." (RH 81)

"I may find myself doing the thing I hate (Romans 7:15). But it really is no longer I who is doing it, but the sin still functioning as a living force in the members of my body (verse 23)." (RH 166)

4. Overcoming sin for the person with the new life is a matter of using your body to retrain the other aspects of your person.

"Learning Christ-likeness is not passive. It is active engagement with and in God. And we act with our bodies. Moreover, this bodily engagement is what lays the foundation in our bodily members for readinesses for holiness, and increasingly removes the readinesses to sin." (GO 90)

Other relevant citations

GO 83: [It] is never true that the habits of sin ... by the new birth.

RH 33: Without the inner "yes" ... is not even a temptation.

RH 33: [Sin] itself ... though we do not actually do it.

RH 119: Those who let God be God ... the inclination to sin.

RH 164: [Because] we are now in the grip of grace ... except insofar as we allow it.

RH 211: So sin, through desire and pride ... wound people can inflict on their soul.

RH 224: To the person who is not ... sin still look good.

SD 115: This new form of life ... but we see it as the uninteresting or disgusting thing it is.

SD 117: In the third stage of personal redemption as a real, psychological process ... automatically.

See also Dallas' article "Beyond Pornography: Spiritual Formation Studied in a Particular Case," *available at dwillard.org.*

Example—Scoring sin

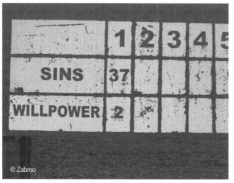

At the top we used the example of a baseball scoreboard: Willpower 2 Sins 37. If you were coaching a team that consistently lost, due to errors, mistakes, poor performance, or bad morale, you probably wouldn't just go into the locker room and yell, "Try harder!" And if you had any love for the members of the team, or if you really wanted them to succeed, you wouldn't call them idiots, or losers, or failures.

Yet when we face the consequences of our own sin, we tend to either blame a lack of willpower or tell ourselves we're lazy scum. Have you ever heard your own voice telling you what a horrible person you are? Or resolving to try harder, over and over again?

Trying harder and berating yourself won't get you to stop sinning. Retraining will. A good baseball coach knows that better players lose less often, so he would go back to training basics, find resources, discover practice techniques, and cheer the team on. It's the same with sin. You have to become a better person—build a better character—if you want to actually overcome the power of sin in your life. That happens through changing the way you think and what you do in all the non-sinning moments of your life. If you concentrate on simply not sinning, you're like a weak batter stepping up to the plate: you're going to strike out more than you run.

Winning the game is not about keeping score, willpower, or trying hard. It is about training to become a better ballplayer.

Relationships

SOCIAL CONTEXT (OR DIMENSION)

Introduction

7

The influence of the reality of our social context—society, education, culture, family, and so forth—is a constant theme in Dallas' work, most noticeably in *Spirit of the Disciplines* and *Knowing God*. He generally referred to that reality with terms such as our *social setting* or *social structures*.

Particularly in *Renovation of the Heart*, Dallas used the terms *social context, social dimension,* and occasionally *social self* very specifically to describe the relational aspect of the human person. As one of the five aspects of the human person, social context (or *dimension*) has the unique role of interface with other persons. That is, no one can interact with you without your social dimension coming into play, and you cannot interact at all without it. Even your relationship with God is inherently social in this sense. Thus, social context is part of you, and under the direction of your soul, rather than separate from you or outside of you.

> ## Definition
>
> Social context, as an aspect of the human self, is the fact of interactivity and the set of relations we have with anyone other than ourselves: family, friends, strangers, and especially God.

Quotes

"The human self requires rootedness in others. This is primarily an ontological matter— a matter of being what we are. It is not just a moral matter, a matter of what ought to be. And the moral aspect of it grows out of the ontological. The most fundamental 'other' for the human is, of course, God himself. God is the ultimate social fact for the human being … But because all are to be rooted in God— and really are, whether they want it or not— our ties to one another cannot be isolated from our shared relationship to him, nor our relationship to him from our ties to one another. Our relations to others cannot be right unless we see those others in their relation to God. Through others he comes to us and we only really find others when we see them in him." (RH 36)

"Spiritual formation, good or bad, is always profoundly social. You cannot keep it to yourself. Anyone who thinks of it as a merely private matter has misunderstood it. Anyone who says, 'It's just between me and God,' or 'What I do is my own business,' has misunderstood God as well as 'me.' Strictly speaking there is nothing 'just between me and God.' For all that is between me and God affects who I am; and that, in turn, modifies my relationship to everyone around me. My relationship to others also modifies me and deeply affects my relationship to God. Hence those relationships must be transformed if I am to be transformed." (RH 182)

Other relevant citations

RH 36: [Being] with others, our social dimension ... the church.

RH 181: When we come to deal ... relationships to others.

RH 187: [In] order to do our part ... assault and withdrawal.

RH 195-97: Here are four major elements in the new world of redeemed relationships. ... The first main element in the transformed social dimension is for individuals to come to see themselves whole, as God himself sees them .... The second element in the spiritually transformed social dimension is abandonment of all defensiveness .... And then all pretense would vanish from our lives. That would be the third element in the spiritually transformed social dimension of the self .... The fourth element is an opening up of our broader social dimension to redemption .... life involvement with others.

Example—John Donne and the body of Christ

"No man is an island, entire of itself; every man is a piece of the continent, a part of the main ... " wrote John Donne. It seems likely that most of us who have heard this line have thought of it as a poetic metaphor. You may have seen it as a way for Donne to speak to his respect for others or his feelings of camaraderie. But if Dallas Willard had written the John Donne Meditation, he would not have been speaking in metaphors, but making an ontological claim: relations among persons are real things that are part of each human person involved.

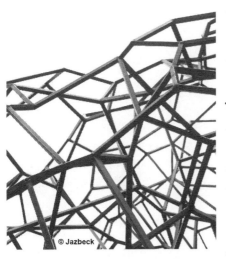
© Jazbeck

Think of the psychological implications: social connections of whatever kind are not *out there* but *in here*. That means that we can no more set aside our relationship to another person than we can set aside our skin or mind: the relationship is actually part of us. So if you thought you could disassociate yourself from your family, leaving the relationship with your departed mother to deal with later, think again. The relationship is part of you, really. It's not going anywhere and it is affecting all the other parts of you, all the time, most especially your soul.

Similarly, many have understood the body of Christ purely as a metaphor for the church. Christ is the body's head—that is, founder and boss—and everyone else a subordinate part of the body—that is, an heir and worker. What might the ontological reality of social connection mean for the way you think of the church, or of Jesus?

SOUL

Introduction

Soul in ordinary social speech commonly denotes something within us that is eternal (maybe), divine (unlikely) and mysterious; it is the real person (contrary to the body) and goes to heaven when we die. The word is often used synonymously with spirit.

None of these, of course, is how Dallas uses it. Perhaps the very nature of the soul lends itself better to metaphor and poetry than to enumeration and definition. In Dallas' work, it is computer, timer, stream, vast landscape, and star.

The soul is one of the five aspects of a human person, along with body, mind, spirit/will/heart, and social context. Unlike the others, it has independent life and substance: souls can exist without body, mind, will, or interaction. Nonetheless, it influences and is influenced by the other four aspects of the person; if they are operating in a healthy way and are connected to God, so will the soul be healthy. When healthy a soul is connected to and enlivened by God's spirit; when damaged it is alienated from God and connected to anything else it can get. The soul loves to be at rest in God, but it is easily distracted or malformed by the other four aspects of the person.

The soul coordinates but does not impel.

The soul is the matriarch of the self—it is the aspect that holds everything else together, without which the other aspects will go their own way. The soul is the conductor of the self, the one with the clearest sense of the symphony, which regulates, coordinates and manages the other players. It is the cohering element of the self that brings the rest together in a unity of operation and purpose, that purpose being one whole life.

But, as with a matriarch or a conductor, if the soul is embittered or broken or distracted, the whole will go to pieces, and eventually will find another cohering authority to organize it. And if the other players are messing up, the soul will be injured as well.

243

Definition

~~The soul is that regulating~~ and coordinating aspect of a person that, when healthy and connected to God, brings the other aspects together as a cooperative system. When the soul is damaged, the other aspects cannot operate as a healthy unit, and will find a different regulating and cohering force. When the soul rests in God, takes its cues from God, and is kept healthy by God, the human person operates as it should—the mind and body working under the auspices of a right spirit, the self in good relation with others. A damaged soul is healed through indirect effort and grace.

Quotes

1.   The soul is that regulating aspect of the self that when healthy and connected to God, brings the other aspects together as a cooperative system.

"[The] route taken both by the most influential Greek thinkers, Plato and Aristotle among them, and by the biblical writers is to take the soul as an entity in its own right. The soul is thought of by them as the source of life within the individual, and simultaneously as its ordering principle." (GO 143)

"Granting significant dissimilarities, it is helpful to think of the soul as the 'computer' that operates all dimensions of the human system by governing and coordinating what goes on in them. It has its own nature, parts, properties, and internal and external relations, as indicated earlier." (GO 144-45)

2.   When the soul is damaged, the other aspects cannot operate as a healthy unit, and will find a different regulating and cohering force.

"Because those who do this do not have a whole soul directing their lives toward good, rooted in God, they allow a 'flow' they find outside themselves to take over their thoughts, feelings, behavior, and social relations. That flow intoxicates them. They absolutize the flow and no longer subject it to ordinary tests of truth, reality, and tried-and-true human values. Thus the winning of a championship by a city team can lead to looting, burning, and death. Romantic/sexual relationship can play the same obsessing role, as can 'success,' leading to workaholic absorption." (RH 203)

3.   When the soul rests in God, takes its cues from God, and is kept healthy by God, the self works as it should—the mind and body working under the auspices of a right spirit, the self in good relation with others.

"In the person with the 'well-kept heart,' the soul will be itself properly ordered under God and in harmony with reality … For such a person, the human spirit will be in correct relationship to God. With his assisting grace, it will bring the soul into subjection to God and the mind (thoughts, feelings) into subjection to the soul. The social context and the body will then come into subjection to thoughts and feelings that are in agreement with truth and with God's intent and purposes for us. Any given event in our life would then proceed as it should, because our soul is functioning properly under God." (RH 199)

4.   A damaged soul is healed through indirect effort and grace.

"[The] indispensable first step in caring for the soul is to place it under God." (RH 208)

"[The soul] can be significantly 'reprogrammed,' and this too is a major part of what goes into the spiritual formation (re-formation) of the person." (RH 37)

Other relevant citations

See *Renovation of the Heart*, page 201, for an exquisite description of the soul's operation and causes of its malformation.

GO 139: [A] soul is essentially a component of a person … that integrates all of the components of his or her life into their life, one life.

GO 143: Although soul is a cosmic principle … including bodily feelings.

RH 202: The human soul is a vast spiritual (nonphysical) landscape … receives his grace.

RH 205: When we speak … power in the human being.

RH 220: [These] are features of life that well up out of a soul that is at home in God …. as God intended.

Example—Dough. Or concrete.

Yet another metaphor. If you don't cook, feel free to insert "cement mixer" and the ingredients of concrete.

© John Morgan

If you have ever used a stand mixer to mix dough, you may have noticed that the flour and water are turned into stretchy stringy glutinous stuff by the operation of the stand mixer and its dough hook. The flour and the water are made into one newish unit. When you add the "extras" like yeast and salt, they are outside the flourwater unit until mixed into it by the dough hook. As the dough hook works, the whole sticky mess turns into a single coherent ball of dough, smooth and soft and full of life.

But woe to anyone whose bowl goes flying off the mixer (as mine has) or whose dough hook is mispositioned (me again) or uses too much of one ingredient: too much water and you have floury gruel; too much salt kills the yeast. The stand mixer can work for hours and never pull it into dough.

The soul is the stand mixer of the person. It needs its partners to be right in order to make the staff of life that bread can be.

246

SPIRIT (OR WILL OR HEART)

Introduction

One of the keys to reading any of Dallas' works is to realize that the words spirit, will, and heart all refer to the same entity (one of five aspects of the human person) but to different senses of that aspect. That is, each term emphasizes a different set of qualities, but they all point to the same reality. There is a classic example of this distinction from the work of philosopher Gottlob Frege: When you say "the morning star" you mean "the last celestial body visible in the morning." When you say "the evening star" you mean "the first celestial body visible in the evening." Whether you say "the morning star" or "the evening star", you are referring to the planet Venus. The sense is different, but the thing referred to is the same.

So it is with *spirit/will/heart*. Same thing, different emphases. It is the part of the human person that connects to God, initiates action, and expresses character. It can be impulsive or reflective, acting from desire or by deliberation. The spirit/will/heart can be embodied, acting from habit for good or ill.

It is the "executive center" of the human person, orienting the whole system (including the soul!), impelling its actions, and keeping it in line. If the spirit/will/heart goes wrong, is damaged, or is poorly formed, the whole self will go wrong. Hence, re-forming the spirit is essential to restoration of the human person. This spiritual re-forming is achieved through consistent practice and wise guidance, also known as discipline.

Definition

The spirit/will/heart is one of the five aspects of the human person, along with mind, body, soul, and social context. It is a nonphysical substance, as God is, but it is not independent; it is part of the soul. Though the three words refer to the same aspect of the human self, the qualities associated with each differ: *Will* emphasizes the aspect's power to initiate, create, choose, or self-determine action. There is a sense of movement, of impetus. *Spirit* emphasizes the aspect's unbodily, nonphysical nature, particularly as it resembles God's Spirit, as well as its intimate connection with the soul. *Heart* emphasizes the aspect's centrality as the characteristic core of the human being, orienting and shaping the person, particularly noticeable in its expression as character.

Quotes

General

"The spirit in man is not the soul, but is the central part of the soul, the power of self-determination. It is the heart or will: the power, embedded in the soul, of choosing. It is that in the human being that must above all be restructured. From it, then, the divine restructuring can be extended to the rest of the life, including the body. For the spirit or will also is the executive center of the self, which—given the birth from above—enables the individual to restructure or reprogram the wrung soul, along with the body, through spiritual disciplines." (GO 156-57)

Will

"Often—perhaps usually—what we do is not an outcome of deliberate choice and a mere act of will, but is more of a relenting to pressure on the will from one or more of the dimensions of the self." (RH 39)

248

"The will, a fundamental dimension of the human soul, can only act from ideas or representations, on the one hand, and emotions or feelings, on the other. It is a power of self-determination, to be sure, and an inherent part of a human soul." (GO 149)

"Vital or *impulsive will* is where you simply choose what you desire, and *reflective will* is where instead of just doing what you want, you choose what is good—and especially, as Christians, what is good under God, in the kingdom of God with Jesus. A crucial third perspective on the will (human spirit) is to see it as *embodied will*. Embodied will is where impulsive will or reflective will has settled into your body to such an extent that you automatically, without prior deliberation, do what they dictate." (*Spiritual Formation and the Warfare Between the Flesh and the Human Spirit*)

Spirit

"We pull all these thoughts together by saying that spirit is *unbodily personal power*. It is primarily a *substance*, and it is above all God, who is both spirit and substance." (DC 81)

"The heart, or will, simply is spirit in human beings. It is the human spirit, and the only thing in us that God will accept as the basis of our relationship to him. It is the spiritual plane of our natural existence, the place of truth before God, from where alone our whole lives become eternal." (DC 81)

Heart

"In biblical language the will is usually referred to as 'heart.' This it is that organizes all the dimensions of personal reality to form a life or a person. The will, or heart, is the executive center of the self. Thus the center point of the spiritual in humans as well as in God is self-determination, also called freedom and creativity." (DC 80-81)

"This does not mean that the whole person actually does only what the heart directs, any more than a whole organization actually does precisely what the chief executive officer (CEO) directs." (RH 30)

"The goodness of the kingdom heart, by contrast, is the positive love of God and of those around us that fills it and crowds out the many forms of evil." (DC 168)

Other relevant citations

DC 82: To understand spirit as "substance" … absolutely so with God.

DC 206: Remember that our heart is our will … entire personality.

GO 53: Spiritual formation in Christ … character of Jesus himself.

GO 73: We teach people to do "all things whatsoever" … the will.

RH 13: You have a spirit … for it to be "formed."

RH 29: Those with a well-kept heart … they manage in life as a whole.

RH 144: It is the core … trust in him.

RH 154: [Habitual] following of a desire … spiritual inertia.

Example—Stand mixers and symphonies

Elsewhere in this dictionary you will find a hodgepodge of metaphors describing the soul and other invisible aspects of the human person. Some are Dallas', some are mine, and most are attempts to distinguish between the spirit/will/heart and the soul. In the entry for *Five (or Six) Aspects of the Human Person* is a diagram Dallas used extensively; on page 40 of *Renovation of the Heart* is another. Both have maddened better students than I, so perhaps diagramming is not a way to go. In the entry for *Soul* I used stand mixers, orchestras, and matriarchs, so in the interest of coherence, here's a stab at spirit/will/heart.

Imagine an orchestra: conductor, musicians, instruments, music stands, sheet music, audience, concert hall. All the parts contribute to the quality of the whole.

The conductor is the soul of the orchestra. The conductor is separate from the orchestra: he or she has a unique task, and could go work for another orchestra. The task of the conductor is to guide and regulate the orchestra, and to keep it on track. The conductor decides tempo, key, overall sound, timing, and so forth, according to his

Novoměstský orchestra (2006)
by Peeca, http://creativecommons.org/licenses/by/3.0, via Wikimedia Commons

or her vision of the music. The conductor can guide the orchestra into beauty or chaos.

The musicians' interactivity with each other, the conductor, and the audience, is the social context. The sheet music, along with the intention and reflection of the people involved, are the mind.

The musicians themselves and the instruments are the body. It takes the musicians and the instruments to make the music and implement the conductor's vision. If they are good, well-trained musicians with excellent instruments, the music should be beautiful. If the instruments are great but the musicians are hacks, the music will show it.

The spirit/will/heart is the activity of the musicians. Not the musicians themselves, but their activity. Some of their activity is habitual, the product of having played and practiced for years: it has become part of the way their bodies operate without thinking. Some of it is impulsive, the product of a physical change (like a sneeze) or a whim. Some of their activity is reflective, the product of thinking through the

251

conductor's vision, the music itself, and the abilities of the instrument, and deliberately implementing it. In a well-rehearsed, disciplined musician, much of the reflective activity has become habitual—embodied—and very little of the impulsive has. The quality of the musicians' activity depends upon the choices they make—both while playing and while living their lives, their physical and mental strength and competence, their discipline, their desire, and the quality and amount of training and formation they have accomplished.

If the conductor (soul) takes a coffee break mid-symphony, the activity of the musicians (spirit/will/heart) will degenerate into chaos, or will pick up another organizing structure (like the drumbeat) altogether. If some of the musicians start playing another tune (the will chooses different ends), or are hungover (the heart is damaged), or stop paying attention to the conductor (the spirit gets distracted), the music will suffer. The conductor might get upset, or lose his mind, or quit. That is, the soul of the orchestra is wrecked.

Then it's up to the audience to react. Pity the poor conductor or musicians who put too much stock in what the audience thinks.

If all goes wrong, it's up to the conductor to get healing and regain vision; the musicians have to pick up their instruments, pay attention, and retrain themselves. If it all goes well, beauty is created and God is glorified.

SPIRITUAL DISCIPLINES

Introduction

A discipline is neither a means of punishment nor behavior in accordance with a set of external rules. A discipline is a planned regular activity meant to improve skills or develop talents. A spiritual discipline is one meant to develop Christlikeness.

Disciplines work indirectly, by "building the muscles" of your character. A pianist practices scales and arpeggios in order to play piano well. Excelling at scales and arpeggios themselves is not the goal; playing piano well is. A disciple practices silence and fasting. Excelling at silence and fasting is not the goal; a character reflective of Christ is. Scales and arpeggios are not punishments (we hope!), and neither are silence and fasting. In fact, Dallas preferred the term *disciplines for the spiritual life*, emphasizing that the practice is meant to make your spiritual life work better.

There are many classical or time-honored spiritual disciplines, but they are not the only ones. A contemporary disciple may find that practicing the discipline of waiting in the longest line in the grocery store curbs his need for instant gratification or control. Dallas suggested that, in our contemporary world, sleep may be a necessary *spiritual* discipline.

This is the set of classical disciplines to which Dallas generally referred: solitude, silence, fasting, frugality, chastity, secrecy, sacrifice (the disciplines of abstinence) and study, worship, celebration, service, prayer, fellowship, confession, submission (the disciplines of engagement). Of the classical disciplines, he most refers to solitude and silence, fasting, worship, prayer, and submission. He also strongly encouraged a discipline of memorizing long passages of Scripture.

253

Definition

A (Christian) spiritual discipline is a planned, regular activity of the body and mind designed to form the spirit. Through disciplines for the spiritual life, along with God's grace, the apprentice develops Christlikeness and an increasing participation in God's kingdom and the divine order.

Quotes

"Spiritual disciplines are activities in our power that we engage in to enable us to do what we cannot do by direct effort. The singing of hymns, for example, is a major spiritual discipline." (GO 52)

" [The] fundamental idea of *growing* in the 'Christ focus' through *specific practices* is absolutely *crucial* to knowing Christ in the contemporary world. Spiritual disciplines are things we can do to increase our receptivity to grace … simply wise ways of opening ourselves to the 'Presence' ever more fully. They are avenues of knowing Christ now." (KCT 159)

Other relevant citations

DC 353: [T]hey are disciplines designed … which is God and his kingdom.

GO 114: For example, if I find, as most do, that I cannot by direct effort succeed … in the moment of need.

SD 68: The disciplines are activities of the mind and body purposefully undertaken … instruments of righteousness unto God."

Exercise—Permission to experiment and play

Spiritual formation in Christlikeness is important, and should be taken seriously but not solemnly. God is a joyful being, and our goal is to be in relationship with God, so we can afford to be joyous and playful. It helps to approach your formation with a sense of experimentation, being dedicated to the process but releasing the outcomes to Jesus.

Spiritual disciplines are not ends in themselves. You don't gain points by doing them well or the same way forever. In fact, the best discipline may be the one you don't need consistently anymore. Since our personalities and circumstance differ, we may have to fiddle with our routines a bit—even get creative!—to find what actually works for us.

If you're an extrovert, try doing something that engages with others. If you are impatient, you might choose the long line at the grocery store and share appropriate jokes with others waiting. If you're an introvert, most of the classic disciplines are right up your alley, but few of us know how to celebrate without throwing a party or overeating. Try marking each little achievement—cleaning your desk, blessing the tailgating driver—with a hearty "Whoopee!" Take a deep breath of peace and joy before you go on to the next task.

Or tinker with longtime practices. If journaling is getting old, try drawing. If you're finally admitting you are not awake enough in the morning to pray, spend a minute breathing in the coffee fumes and consecrating the brew before you drink. Read the same psalm every day at the same time, steeping in the language and imagery, rather than reading 150 of them in 150 days.

Stick with a new discipline for at least thirty consecutive days, then evaluate its utility based on how you are responding in the world, rather than whether you're "succeeding" at the activity itself. Most of all, enjoy the time you spend with your self and with God. You were made for his "en-joyment."

SPIRITUAL FORMATION (IN CHRIST)

Introduction

Spiritual formation is, quite literally, the forming or shaping of one's spirit. Remember that your spirit is a substance: it will be unintentionally shaped and formed by your experiences, thoughts, feelings, habits and fulfilled desires. Rather than letting the world treat your spirit like modeling clay, you can influence what shape it becomes. You may choose to intentionally form your spirit, with God's grace, into one that looks like that of Christ.

The process of spiritual formation is the process of reclaiming all our elements for the Kingdom of God. That's what the disciplines are for, working with the action of God.

The goal of spiritual formation is transformation. The transformation comes from God. Your role is to make space for it, and, through intention and discipline, to train your inner self to accept that grace.

Definition

Spiritual formation in Christ is the intentional process to shape a person's inner being to be like the inner being of Christ: God-connected, self-denying, joyful, easily obedient. While spiritual formation is always dependent upon the leadership of the Spirit and the provision of God's grace, it is founded on intentional human efforts.

Quotes

1.   Spiritual formation in Christ is the intentional process to shape a person's inner being to be like the inner being of Christ: God-connected, self-denying, joyful, easily obedient.

"Spiritual formation for the Christian basically refers to the Spirit-driven process of forming the inner world of the human self in such a way that it becomes like the inner being of Christ himself." (RH 22)

257

"Everyone receives spiritual formation, just as everyone gets an education. The only question is whether it is a good one or a bad one. We need to take a conscious, intentional hand in the developmental process." (GO 69)

2.   While spiritual formation is always dependent upon the leadership of the Spirit and the provision of God's grace, it is founded on intentional human efforts.

"Spiritual formation is the process through which those who love and trust Jesus Christ effectively take on his character. When this process is what it should be, they increasingly live their lives as he would if he were in their place ... This process of 'conformation to Christ,' as we might more appropriately call it, is constantly supported by grace and otherwise would be impossible. But it is not therefore passive. Grace is opposed to earning, not to effort. In fact, nothing inspires and enhances effort like the experience of grace." (GO 80)

Other relevant citations

GO 16: "Spiritual formation" ... and transparently flow.

RH 22: [Spiritual] formation for the Christian ... inner being of Christ himself.

RH 23: The instrumentalities ... It is, finally, a gift of grace.

RH 77: Spiritual formation in Christ is ... God's present and eternal kingdom.

Example—The devil's music

European medievals christened the tritone—a dissonant chord— "the devil in music." In the 1920s, jazz musician Jelly Roll Morton revealed that his grandmother had tried to turn him away from that "devil music." The blues, derived from Black gospel, was demonized for luring good Christians out of the church and into the juke joint, where sinful activity was sure to happen.

©Marcin Wichery

And if you are of a certain age, you will remember the scandal over the idea that one could play a Beatles LP in reverse and hear satanic language.

You may not buy the idea that some music is immoral and some not. Or that reality television is evil and PBS is wholesome. Still, there is no question that the way we think and what we think about is shaped by what enters our heads. If you are always around negative people, you are more likely to think negative thoughts. If your music is filled with four-letter words and degrading imagery your mind will spend more time with those words and images than if not. For that matter, if you are reading a lot of academic books that use eight-syllable words, your papers will send up shoots of obscurity when you're not looking.

We are formed by choice or by accident. If you want your spirit to be formed to be like Christ, one of the first places to examine is wherever it is you put your mind when you're not using it. In my own case, when I notice I am becoming cynical I fast from radio news.

Dallas used to hum hymns to himself and quote them during speeches, not leaving much room left for the devil to make music of his own.

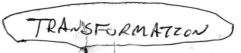

SPIRITUAL LIFE AND SPIRITUAL PERSON

Introduction

The only challenge to understanding Dallas' notion of the spiritual life is the contemporary parlance of spirituality. The spiritual life isn't the activities you *do,* even if you do them because you're "spiritual" — that is, capable of extra-normal experience. Nor is *spiritual* a synonym for *not religious.* A spiritual life is a life lived in the power and influence of the Spirit. It is your life lived in the present Kingdom of God. We are all essentially spiritual, so in that sense there are no non-spiritual people. Being a *spiritual person* is about one's life being spiritual—that is, integrated into and driven by the Holy Spirit. The spiritual person is one whose spirit is being shaped, formed, and renewed by God.

Notice that this definition—life lived in the power and influence of the Spirit—requires no mystical or transcendent experience. One has a spiritual life, because one's life is organized around the Spirit of God, who interacts with every aspect of life.

The specifically *spiritual* life of a spiritual person is not distinct from that person's non-spiritual life; it is his whole life that is filled with the Spirit. So spiritual life, per se, is not about any prescribed set of actions: neither lighting incense and chanting, nor being in a pew from 11-12 on Sunday morning. But order and intention of action are important training mechanisms for the spiritual life.

Definition

The spiritual life is one's own real life, lived in interactive personal relationship with God. At its best, all five aspects of the human person are flooded with life from God, are focused on and organized around him, and are empowered and sustained by him.

A spiritual person is one whose every aspect of life is integrated into and dominated by the Spirit. There is a scale: the more one's life is lived in the Kingdom, the more spiritual one is.

Quotes

1. The spiritual life is one's own real life, lived in interactive personal relationship with God.

"In the Christian version of personalized spirit and spirituality, the spiritual life takes on the character of a personal relationship between individuals, with the attendant features of reciprocal attention, care, provision, assistance or service, emotional interaction, expectations, comfort, joy, and development or growth … On one side there is a transcendental spiritual being, God, with his retinue and his realm or governance, and on the other side human beings, individually and in groups, all together constituting what is called 'The Kingdom of God.'" (*Spirituality for Smarties*)

"Those who really do know Christ in the modern world do so by seeking and entering the kingdom of God … . To know Christ in the modern world is to know him in your world now. To know him in your world now is to live interactively with him right where you are in your daily activities. This is the spiritual life in Christ." (KCT 139)

"[Spiritual] life is a matter of living our lives from the reality of God." (GO 51)

2. At its best, all five aspects of the human person are flooded with life from God, are focused on and organized around him, and are empowered and sustained by him.

"The ideal of the spiritual life in the Christian understanding is one where all of the essential parts of the human self are effectively organized around God, as they are restored and sustained by him." (RH 31)

"We are, all of us, never-ceasing spiritual beings with a unique eternal calling to count for good in God's great universe." (DC 21)

"We are hindered in our progress toward becoming spiritually competent people by how easily we can explain away the movements of God toward us ... for now he cooperates with the desires and inclinations that make up our character as we are gradually becoming the kind of people we will forever be ... . Only a very hardy individualist or social rebel—or one desperate for another life—therefore stands any chance of discovering the substantiality of the spiritual life today ... [All areas of life in which we can become spiritually competent] require of us a choice to be a spiritual person, to live a spiritual life. We are required to 'bet our life' that the visible world, while real, is not reality itself ... " (HG 217-20)

Other relevant citations

DC 79: For it is in persons ... or feel about it.

DC 82-83: Because we are spiritual beings ... no longer dependent in any way upon the physical.

GO 112: The human being ... is a spiritual person.

KCT 153-54: [The] context of *his* action where we know the eternal life flowing in us and around us ... is the spiritual life in Christ.

SD 67: A person is ... under God is not yet achieved.

Example—Spirituality for atheists

In a recent blog post entitled "In Awe of Everything," author Adam Lee (*Daylight Atheism*) acknowledged that many professed atheists speak of spirituality or of being spiritual. Lee sorted out what they might mean when they say they are spiritual, partly on the basis of spiritual atheists' descriptions of their feelings during a spiritual experience. As he puts it, spirituality for an atheist consists in the experience of awe and wonder, or a sense of the sacred and reverence for deeper aspects of life. For Lee, being spiritual is a psychological state.

For Dallas, being spiritual is a recognition that the deeper aspects of the world *are* spiritual. Spirituality is not about being spiritual, but being a spiritual being. To use a word from philosophy, "spiritual" is an ontological category, not a psychological state. You are a spiritual being; you cannot help but be spiritual. Where the two definitions overlap is in their acknowledgement that being open to awe and wonder is critical to living and deepening a spiritual life.

SPIRITUAL REALITY

Introduction

The term *spiritual reality* might be better written as a statement: reality is spiritual. This is not to deny the real presence of a visible, material world. But the foundational reality, the *real* beyond and behind and throughout the finite material world, is spiritual and nonphysical.

Spiritual reality contains spiritual beings. God is, of course, the primary spiritual being, but such creatures as angels are spiritual and wholly real. Insofar as we choose to live out of our spiritual nature, we too are spiritual beings living in a spiritual reality.

> ## Definition
>
> Spiritual reality is the hidden —because nonphysical— ultimate and powerful foundation of the visible, material and finite universe. It is the "where" of spiritual beings. It is the kingdom of God.

Quotes

"[It] is in persons, or 'selves' — and their experiences of feeling, thought, and will— that we primarily come to know precisely what the spiritual is. 'Spiritual' is not just something we ought to be. It is something we are and cannot escape, regardless of how we may think or feel about it. It is our nature and our destiny." (DC 79)

"[T]he *biblical* conception of the spiritual is that of an *ordered realm of personal power* founded in the God who is himself spirit and not a localizable physical body .... The biblical worldview also regards the spiritual as a realm fundamental to the existence and behavior of *all* natural or physical reality. And it is one in which people may participate by engaging it through the active life tendency called 'faith' ... " (SD 64-65)

"The visible world daily bludgeons us with its things and events. They pinch and pull and hammer away at our bodies. Few people arise in the morning as hungry for God as they are for cornflakes and eggs. But instead of shouting and shoving, the spiritual world whispers at us ever so gently. And it appears both at the edges and in the middle of events and things in the so-called real world of the visible … . the tendency of life in Christ is progressively toward the inward word to the receptive heart. The aim is to move entirely into the hidden realm of spiritual reality … " (HG 217-20)

Other relevant citations

GO 112: In the Christian context … Outside that context there are, of course, other spirits.

KCT 123: Since there is such a vast … of religion and the Bible.

SD 66: [Though Adam and Eve didn't suffer physical death] they nevertheless died … and the Spirit against them.

Exercise—Populating spiritual reality

Take a moment to absorb all this. You are a spiritual and material being, living in a material world, which is part of a much larger material universe, which is part of a much larger spiritual reality, populated by spiritual beings both like and unlike you, as well as by God.

Perhaps this is not news. You may already believe in demons and angels, or ghosts and banshees and wraiths. You may already believe in God and a spiritual heaven that somehow also has streets of gold. But for just a moment, *see* your room filled to the brim with spiritual beings, and somehow also filled with God, along with the books, papers, furniture, and general flotsam. Notice that not only is your room replete with all this, but it also is overflowing with Glory, as is every part of the material and nonmaterial universe.

Write down what spiritual beings you actually believe in. You may not believe in angels, or may think there are at most a dozen or so. You may not believe in a supremely evil spiritual creature, called Satan or the Devil or Beelzebub, but absolutely believe in evil. You may not believe in demons, or not believe that they are in a cosmic battle with us. You may believe only in God, and not really even be sure about that one, and

266

certainly be skeptical about the Trinity. Whatever you believe, write it down, and then mentally populate whatever you think reality is with those creatures.

Meditate on Psalm 8, which gives a glimpse of the vast and close realness of spiritual reality:

> O Lord, our Lord, how excellent is Your name in all the earth, who have set Your glory above the heavens!

> Out of the mouth of babes and nursing infants You have ordained strength, because of Your enemies, that You may silence the enemy and the avenger.

> When I consider Your heavens, the work of Your fingers, the moon and the stars, which You have ordained, what is man that You are mindful of him, and the son of man that You visit him? For You have made him a little lower than the angels, and You have crowned him with glory and honor. You have made him to have dominion over the works of Your hands; You have put all things under his feet, all sheep and oxen—even the beasts of the field, the birds of the air, and the fish of the sea that pass through the paths of the seas.

> O Lord, our Lord, how excellent is Your name in all the earth! (NKJV)

SPIRITUAL TRANSFORMATION (OR TRANSFORMATION INTO CHRISTLIKENESS)

Introduction

Easy obedience to Christ is the goal of discipleship, but this cannot be achieved by external obedience to God's law, nor by the power of the will to refrain from some acts and commit others. In fact, even concentrated work to train your will (or spirit or heart) is not enough: training your spirit alone will not result in obedience, because your spirit will be battling against habits of the body and mind. Willpower doesn't make for holiness. Change does.

Easy obedience to Christ comes along with transformation into Christlikeness. That is, as the nonphysical aspects of the human person increasingly resemble the nonphysical aspects of Christ, so will the person's physical acts resemble Christ's. Hence, easy obedience to Christ is the result of transformation of all the aspects of the inner self into Christlikeness. This is what *spiritual transformation* is, and what Dallas (somewhat misleadingly) referred to as the *renovation of the heart*.

> ### Definition
>
> Spiritual transformation is the transformation of all aspects of the human self into Christlikeness. It results in easy obedience to Christ, joyous devotion to God, and a life wholly lived in the kingdom of the heavens.

Quotes

1. Spiritual transformation is the transformation of all aspects of the human self into Christlikeness.

"Spiritual transformation into Christlikeness, I have said, is the process of forming the inner world of the human self in such a way that it takes on the character of the inner being of Jesus himself … becomes a natural expression of the inner reality of Jesus and of his teachings.

Doing what he said and did increasingly becomes a part of who we are." (RH 159)

"[The] aim of spiritual formation is the transformation of the self, and that it works through transformation of thought, transformation of feeling, transformation of social relations, transformation of the body, and transformation of the soul. When we work with all these, transformation of the spirit (heart, will) very largely, though not entirely, takes care of itself." (GO 60)

2.   It results in easy obedience to Christ, joyous devotion to God, and a life wholly lived in the kingdom of the heavens.

"The outcome of spiritual formation is, indeed, the transformation of the inner reality of the self in such a way that the deeds and words of Jesus become a natural expression of who we are." (RH 165)

"Single-minded and joyous devotion to God and his will, to what God wants for us-and to service to him and to others because of him-is what the will transformed into Christlikeness looks like." (RH 143)

Other relevant citations

GO 116: The gifts of the Spirit can only be ... ongoing transformation of the inner being.

RH 22: Christian spiritual formation ... essential outcome ...

RH 41: [Spiritual] transformation only happens ... on the will (heart, spirit) alone.

RH 89: Then the vision and the solid intention to obey ... and character.

RH 215: One whose aim is anything less ... into Christlikeness.

Example—Eating lamb with lemon

How do we do what Jesus did? Become the kind of people that he was. How can we become like Christ? By following him into the overall style and pattern of life he chose for himself. We ask ourselves, "What did he do when he was not doing something remarkable?" We discover that he chose a life of activities that would keep him in constant relationship with God his father.

©Andrew Comings

Being the kind of creatures we are, we tend to imitate the surface activities. So if Jesus forgave his tormentors, we try to be pleasant to those who pester us. If Jesus anointed those he healed, we want to find meaning in the oil itself so to be diligent about doing what he did. I suppose that if archeologists discovered that Jesus ate his lamb with lemon, we'd be doing chemical studies to understand the alchemy of lamb and lemon.

But what gave Jesus the ability to forgive, heal, trust, teach, and all those other remarkable things he did wasn't his divine nature or the trivial accoutrements of a first century life. It was keeping in constant relationship with God, which he achieved by God's grace and by focusing his life on prayer, worship, study, community, and attending to his spirit through silence, solitude, fasting, and so forth every day, and every minute of every day.

STAGES OF APPRENTICESHIP IN JESUS (OR DIMENSIONS OF THE ETERNAL KIND OF LIFE)

Introduction

In chapter nine of *The Divine Conspiracy* Dallas describes five progressive dimensions of the eternal kind of life. This description has echoes of the spiritual progression seen in the structure of the Sermon on the Mount, as described in chapter five.

It can be helpful to think of these dimensions as loose stages, because, as a progression, they describe what happens as we pursue Christlikeness and spend more and more of our lives in the present kingdom of the heavens.

In talks, Dallas also provided a condensed description of this progression, which might be called the *three dimensions of discipleship*.

Definition

The five progressive dimensions (or stages) of the life of an apprentice are: trust in Jesus, desire to be his apprentice, obedience, inner transformation, and finally, the character and power to do the work of the kingdom.

Quotes

"We should be aware of, roughly, five dimensions of our eternal kind of life in The Kingdom Among Us, and these dimensions more or less arrange themselves in the following progression:

1. *Confidence in and reliance upon Jesus* as 'the Son of man,' the one appointed to save us … This confidence is a reality, and it is itself a true manifestation of the 'life from above,' not of normal human capacities …

2. But this confidence in the person of Jesus naturally leads to a *desire to be his apprentice* in living in and from the kingdom of God … .

3. The abundance of life realized through apprenticeship to Jesus, 'continuing in his word, naturally leads to *obedience* ... Love of Jesus sustains us through the course of discipline and training that makes obedience possible. Without that love, we will not stay to learn.

4. Obedience, with the life of discipline it requires, both leads to and, then, issues from the *pervasive inner transformation of the heart and soul* ... as we admire and emulate Jesus and do whatever is necessary to learn how to obey him.

5. Finally, there is *power to work the works of the kingdom* ... Great power requires great character if it is to be a blessing and not a curse, and that character is something we only grow toward." (DC 366-68)

"The various scenes and situations that Jesus discusses in his Discourse on the Hill are actually stages in a progression toward a life of agape love. They progressively presuppose that we know where our well-being really lies, that we have laid aside anger and obsessive desire, that we do not try to mislead people to get our way, and so on. Then loving and helping those who hurt us and hate us, for example, will come as a natural progression." (DC 139)

Exercise—The Discourse on the Hill

In *The Divine Conspiracy*, Dallas wrote that Matthew 5-7, known as the *Sermon on the Mount* or the *Discourse on the Hill*, demonstrated the spiritual progression toward agape love that comes with apprenticeship. He suggested that doing what Jesus talks about later in the Discourse depends upon being the kind of person he describes earlier in the discourse: one cannot hear and implement the teaching about anger and contempt (Mt. 5:21-26) without having first assimilated the teaching about well-being found in the Beatitudes.

Try steeping in the Discourse, absorbing its meaning and its structure. Meditate upon how the guidance of the latter parts assumes the learning of the earlier. Then try attaching the Discourse to the progression outlined above, asking "How does the structure of the apprentice's progression provide some framework on which to hang the admonitions of the Discourse? Or does it?"

274

SUBSTANCE

Introduction

To be clear, *substance* isn't a Willardian word, but a philosophical one used in a technical sense throughout formal philosophy. Dallas uses the word *substance* in three distinguishable ways: 1) in the philosophical way, to refer to a basic building block of reality; 2) in the material way, to refer to the physical matter of an object or person; and 3) in a linguistic way, to refer to the gist of an argument.

The latter two—substance as physical matter or as the point of a discussion—are common uses. For example, in *Spirit of the Disciplines*, Dallas wrote that in the Bible the word flesh means both the physical *substance* and a range of powers. In *The Divine Conspiracy* he challenges those who speak for Christ to examine the likely consequences of someone's believing the *substance* of their message. It is the philosophical meaning of *substance* that can flummox the reader. That is the definition provided below.

Definition of philosophical *substance*

Substance is a basic building block of reality, not just material or physical reality, but of all kinds of reality, including spiritual reality. *Substance* refers to the essence, the non-negotiable "stuff" of a thing. A substance is the non-material aspect of a thing that exists no matter what descriptions or properties of the thing change. It is the *je ne sais quoi* of an idea, object, or person.

Quotes

"We pull all these thoughts together by saying that spirit is *unbodily personal power*. It is primarily a *substance*, and it is above all God, who is both spirit and substance." (DC 81)

"To understand spirit as 'substance' is of the utmost importance in our current world, which is so largely devoted to the ultimacy of matter. It means that spirit is something that exists in its own right—to some degree in the human case, and absolutely so with God. Thoughts, feelings, willings, and their developments are so many dimensions of this spiritual substance, which exercises a power that is outside the physical. Space is occupied by it, and it may manifest itself there as it chooses." (DC 82)

"The soul is, as Professor Moreland indicates, a substance, in the sense that it is an individual entity that has properties and dispositions natural to it, endures through time and change, and receives and exercises causal influence on other things, most notably the person of which it is the most fundamental part." (GO 138)

Example—Square and cat

What is the substance of "square"? What does it have to have to be a square? This one is easy, because we use the word *square* to name a particular abstract idea. A square is a two-dimensional object having four 90° corners and four sides of equal length. No matter what else you can say about any particular square (green, big, rotating, solid), it cannot be a square without those three characteristics.

What is the substance of "cat"? What must a thing have to be properly called a *cat?* We begin by asking, "what can it not do without and remain a cat?" Is it a tail? Whiskers? Meow? None of these is the substance of cat, because we can easily imagine a cat with neither tail nor whiskers, and that cannot meow.

Cats are carnivorous and have fur, but could a vegetarian hairless thing, however pathetic, be a cat? Sure—you may have met just such a creature.

The substance of "cat" is not physical, not material, and perhaps is indescribable. But whatever it is that makes a thing a "cat" is its substance. Whatever it is that makes a thing a cat is its indivisible, unchanging essence, uniquely common to anything one might call a cat.

That essence affects other creatures and its environment in a way that a cat's less essential characteristics (color, hair quality, diet) do not.

So, to say that spirit is a substance means that it is an indivisible unchanging essence in itself—it exists, period, and is not derived from anything else.

Exercise—The substance of God

Read a Bible passage that describes God; Psalm 89 and Job 9:4-11 are good choices. Scratch out each description or adjective or action of God. What do you have left? Is that the essence of God? Now look at Exodus 3:13-15, in which God reveals God's name as "I AM." Pure, uncreated existence: is that closer to God's substance?

Take a moment to describe whatever it is about God you find most essential to your understanding. What could you be wrong about without your "losing" God?

Resources for further exploration

Robinson, Howard, "Substance", The Stanford Encyclopedia of Philosophy (Winter 2009 Edition), Edward N. Zalta (ed.), available at http://plato.stanford.edu. This is an excellent summary of some of the most important historical discussions of the idea of substance, including those by Aristotle, Hume, Locke, and Strawson. Though it's not an easy read, it is a lot easier than reading the philosophers themselves! If you read nothing else in this essay, read the discussion of Aristotle's *Categories*, the book that started it all.

Ayers, M.R., "The Ideas of Power and Substance in Locke's Philosophy", The Philosophical Quarterly, Vol. 25, No. 98 (Jan., 1975), 1-27. Ayers' analysis of Locke includes discussion of both "power" and "substance". Both of these terms are essential to understanding Dallas' writings, and Locke is one of Dallas' strongest influences in this.

Dallas' article "Intentionality and the Substance of the Self", written for the Society of Christian Philosophers meeting, American Philosophical Association, San Francisco. April 4, 2007; available at dwillard.org. This article connects Dallas' understanding of both physical and spiritual substance, the self, and how we come to do what we do. It is reasonably accessible, and would add depth to the reader's understanding of *The Divine Conspiracy*, for example.

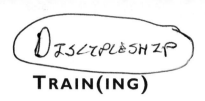

TRAIN(ING)

Introduction

If you have ever had the experience of wanting to do something but not being able to do it … welcome to being human! Nearly from the moment of our birth we have desires but don't have the abilities to match. Infants want to eat, but have to wait for help. Teenagers want to drive but have to learn how first. Adults want to bench press their body weight but can't lift a sack of sugar. And so it goes. From our greatest aspirations to our simplest wants, ability dictates capability. At least at the beginning.

If we want to do something badly enough we may put in the effort needed to learn how to do it. We call that effort *training*. Training is not simple learning of facts: you can know how the accelerator and the steering wheel and the brake work and still run into a tree. Training is not simply trying: you can repeatedly try to lift a heavy barbell and have no success. Training is getting your body and mind, through intentional repetition of planned activity over time, to do what they would not otherwise be able to do.

This is the reason that training for spiritual transformation is a better strategy for consistent obedience to God than using willpower to obey the rules.

Definition

Training is the deliberate undertaking of a course of attitude and practice likely to develop the skills and automatic responses needed to do something one would not otherwise be able to do, or cannot do by direct effort. Training in Christlikeness is necessary to become the kind of person who can do what Jesus commanded easily, consistently, and automatically.

Quotes

1.   Training is the deliberate undertaking of a course of attitude and practice likely to develop the skills and automatic responses needed to do something one would not otherwise be able to do, or cannot do by direct effort.

"Often when we come to do the right thing we have already done the wrong thing, because that is what was sitting in our body 'at the ready.' Intention alone cannot suffice in most situations where we find ourselves. We must be 'in shape.' If not, trying will normally be too late, or totally absent. Instead, our intention and effort must be carried into effect by training which leaves our body poised to do what Christ would do, well before the occasion arises. Such training is supplied by the disciplines for life in the Spirit." (GO 85)

"The training required to transform our most basic habits of thought, feeling, and action will not be done for us." (DC 345)

"[The] body can acquire a 'life of its own'—tendencies to behave without regard to our conscious intentions. In our fallen world this life is prepossessed by evil, so that we do not have to think to do what is wrong, but must think and plan and practice—and receive grace—if we are to succeed in doing what is right." (GO 89)

2.   Training in Christlikeness is necessary to become the kind of person who can do what Jesus commanded easily, consistently, and automatically.

"[If] I intend to obey Jesus Christ, I must intend and decide to become the kind of person who would obey. That is, I must find the means of receiving his grace and changing my inner being until it is substantially like his, pervasively characterized by his thoughts, feelings, habits, and relationship to the Father. Overall, this will amount to a life organized around wise spiritual disciplines under grace. We learn that we cannot do what we should do just by trying, but that by training we can become the kind of person who would do it with little thought or effort. ... A primary objective in training in Christlikeness is to break the power of our ready responses to do the opposite of what Jesus teaches: for example, scorn, anger, verbal manipulation, payback, silent collusion in the wrongdoing of others around us, and so forth. (*Living a Transformed Life Adequate to Our Calling*)

"For example, if I find, as most do, that I cannot by direct effort succeed in 'blessing those who curse me' or 'praying without ceasing,' in putting anger aside or not indulging the covetous or lustful eye, then it is my responsibility to find out how I can train myself (always under grace and divine guidance, we must never forget) so that I will be able to do what I cannot do just by trying in the moment of need." (GO 114)

Other relevant citations

GO 88: We enter into each of the teachings ... for behavior and life are not mental.

GO 171: Much of what we learn in human life is imposed ... no matter what parents and teachers may wish for.

RH 32: The very purpose of learning ... of its own.

SD 7: Jesus never expected us ... comes at the point where it is hard not to respond as he would.

Example—How do you get to Carnegie Hall?

There's a very old joke about a visitor to New York stopping a native on the street to ask for directions to the exalted performance venue known as Carnegie Hall. The visitor asks, "How do you get to Carnegie Hall?" The native responds, "Practice, my friend, practice."

If you didn't know better, you might think that playing Beethoven's Fifth Symphony just meant you needed to sit down on a piano bench with the sheet music and move your fingers on the piano keys. But you know better. You know that playing Beethoven on the piano requires exercising your fingers and your eyes and ears and hands and arms and body and mind over time in ways that seem to have nothing to do with the Fifth Symphony. You don't play Beethoven. You practice scales and arpeggios and key changes. What you're doing when you practice all those exercises to learn piano is systematically changing the muscle memory of your body to move your hands in specific ways, quickly and thoughtlessly and much more effortlessly.

It's the same with living like Christ—being the kind of person Jesus was. If you didn't know better you might think that you could just do what Jesus did—raise the dead, heal the sick, or even something as small as being kind to those who hate you—the first time you tried. But you can't, no matter how hard you try, and God doesn't expect you to. What God does expect is that you will *train* to become the kind of person who *can* be kind to those who hate you, and that over time, with God's compassion and grace, you will be able to be kind without having to think about it.

Raising the dead comes later, right after Carnegie Hall.

TREASURE(S)

Introduction

There is a sweetness to Dallas' use of the word *treasure*. The word itself refers to those people or things or ideas or feelings that we value, and because we value them, try to keep safe. But when he mentions them, particularly in chapter six of *The Divine Conspiracy*, his deep respect for the precious nature of *anyone's* treasures shines through. Tenderness floods his examples of children's treasures and God's treasures. This is as it should be: because treasures are whatever it is that we hold dear, they are clasped by a most vulnerable part of our hearts. We should view others as treasure, and their treasures as precious. We would do well to become aware of what it is we treasure, and to place our "treasurings" on worthy things.

We are God's treasures. That means that we are cherished and protected by God. Knowing this and believing it is what enables us to treasure all God's other treasures.

Definition

Treasures are the things or people we cherish, protect or keep because we put value on them. Our response to their value to us is a function of the will/spirit/heart. This is why "where your treasure is there your heart will be also" (Mt. 6:21) and why we must choose what it is we treasure.
We are God's treasures. Ours is life lived in the kingdom and power of Jesus.

Quotes

1.   Treasures are the things or people we cherish, protect or keep because we put value on them.

"Treasures are things we try to keep because of a value we place upon them. They may be of no value whatsoever in themselves; nevertheless, we take great pains to protect such things. Thus we are said to treasure them … Of course we may also treasure things other than material goods: for example, our reputation, or our relationship to another person, another person, or the security or reputation of our school or our business or our country …. Everyone has treasures. This is an essential part of what it is to be human." (DC 203)

2.   Our response to their value to us is a function of the will/spirit/heart. This is why "where your treasure is there your heart will be also" and why we must choose what it is we treasure.

"Treasures are directly connected to our spirit, or will, and thus to our dignity as persons …. to discuss our treasures is really to discuss our treasuring;. We are not to pass it off as dealing merely with 'external goods,' which are 'nonspiritual' or just physical stuff. It is to deal with the fundamental structure of our soul. It has to do precisely with whether the life we live now in the physical realm is to be an eternal one or not, and the extent to which it will be so." (DC 203-04)

3.   We are God's treasures. Ours is life lived in the kingdom and power of Jesus.

"[Those] who love and are loved by God are not allowed to cease to exist, because they are God's treasures. He delights in them and intends to hold onto them. He has even prepared for them an individualized eternal work in his vast universe … And there God will preserve every one of his treasured friends in the wholeness of their personal existence precisely because he treasures them in that form." (DC 84-85)

"[When] I treasure those around me and see them as God's creatures designed for his eternal purposes, I do not make an additional point of not hating them or calling them twerps or fools. Not doing those things is simply a part of the package." (DC 155)

"[The] treasure is the life and power of Jesus Christ." (GO 50)

Other relevant citations

DC 203: The most important commandment … as he treasures them.
DC 205-06: Thus, to "lay up treasures in heaven" … within God's eternal life.

284

DC 207: We cannot but serve our treasures ... no one escapes.

SD 194: To *trust* in riches ... we will also love them and come to serve them.

Example—Foster parents

Frequently it is said that being a foster parent is a calling, not an activity or a job. Parenting is hard in and of itself; parenting another's child adds layers of concern and challenge. Unlike birth or adoption, there is little anticipation or lead time. A child and his spiritual, emotional, and intellectual baggage are deposited in your care. For the child to flourish, he must be important to you instantly, and you must resolve to care for him immediately, cherishing him as if he were your own beloved son. The child has to become your treasure for as long as he is with you, and when he leaves and the next one comes, she must become your treasure. Regardless of how you feel, you must choose to treasure, because if you do not, your habits of speech and will are likely to damage a soul that has already borne a burden. Hence it is a calling, not a job.

The same may be said for all Jesus' followers in their interactions with other people and with God. Jesus' followers have been given the calling to treasure God and others—or God in others—because of the love and treasuring they have received from God. Treasuring—that is, protecting, caring for, and advancing—isn't a commandment or an activity or a task. It is a calling, and the way of living for the apprentices of Jesus.

TRUST

Introduction

We might say things like, "I trust Terry to complete this work" but then regularly check in on Terry just to be sure. We tell our children, "I trust you," and think we mean it, but find ourselves putting training wheels on their freedom. Among and within us is a powerful skepticism that undermines the *believing* that is a part of trust.

We might distinguish between trusting *that* and trusting *in*. There's a qualitative difference between trusting that our children will be home by 10 and trusting in our children. Trusting *that* is more like assenting that a certain statement is highly likely to be true: "I trust that my child will be home by 10" may say very little about our relationship with the child, but a lot about her chaperone, or the bus she's on, or the training we have given her. But "I trust (*in*) my child" suggests an interactive relationship based on knowledge and past experience.

In this deeper sense, trust has an element of *entrusting*—a giving over of a treasure for safekeeping—or *surrender*. When you trust your child, you are surrendering your powers of approval and interference.

Trusting Jesus, therefore, is different than trusting *that* Jesus *did thus and so*. When you trust (*in*) him, you are entrusting your treasures to him, including your treasured willful self-determination.

> ## Definition
>
> To trust is to entrust or surrender one's treasures, ideally based on the knowledge that comes with an interactive relationship. In the case of trusting Jesus, our treasure is our selves.

Quotes

"Perhaps the hardest thing for sincere Christians to come to grips with is the level of real unbelief in their own life: the unformulated skepticism about Jesus that permeates all dimensions of their being and undermines what efforts they do make toward Christlikeness. The idea that you can trust Christ and not intend to obey him is an illusion generated by the prevalence of an unbelieving 'Christian culture.' In fact, you can no more trust Jesus and not intend to obey him than you could trust your doctor and your auto mechanic and not intend to follow their advice. If you don't intend to follow their advice, you simply don't trust them. Period." (RH 88)

"[The] gospel of the entire New Testament is that you can have new life now in the Kingdom of God if you will trust Jesus Christ. Not just something he did, or something he said, but trust the whole person of Christ in everything he touches—which is everything." (GO 61)

"But to know Christ in the kingdom of God we must abandon ourselves to a total transformation of *who we are on the inside*, to taking on the character of Christ through living with him day by day by day and hour by hour. Only that is trust in Christ." (KCT 152)

"Jesus is actually looking for people he can trust with his power." (GO 16)

Other relevant citations

RH 68: To take him as our master means … One who judges righteously …

SD 194: [W]e *can* possess without using or trusting … unhappy people on earth.

Exercise—Who do you trust?

Dallas used the examples of trusting an auto mechanic to suggest repairs. His idea was that if you take your care to your auto mechanic for repair, and your mechanic recommends a course of action, and—assuming you have the resources—you choose not to do it, the fact is that either you do not trust your auto mechanic or you had no intention of following her advice. If you say that you trust your auto mechanic, but take your car for repair with no intention of doing what she suggests, you actually do not trust your mechanic (though you may enjoy wasting her time). By analogy, if you say you trust Jesus but do not intend to follow his direction, you actually do not trust Jesus.

Examining your trust can be instructive. For example, you might trust your bartender to listen well and give good advice, but not trust him to make a proper drink. You might trust your auto mechanic to be honest, but not to be competent at repairs. Again by analogy, you might trust Jesus to get you into heaven, but not trust that he actually knew what he was talking about on anything else … ? Really?

As an exercise, figure out who you trust and what for. You might want to start with someone peripherally in your life, like the bagger at your grocery store, then work your way up the relationship ladder, through friends, children, partners, bosses, and so forth, up to and including Jesus. Ask yourself: "Do I trust my partner? In what areas? Why not the others?" If you're not sure whether you trust someone, look at your behavior and draw conclusions.

Once you've got a sense of your trust and trust issues, decide what you intend to do about it. Then follow your own advice, if you trust yourself.

TRUTH

Introduction

"What is truth?" Pontius Pilate infamously asked. His (probably rhetorical) question was asked in response to Jesus' assertion that "the reason I was born and came into the world is to testify to the truth. Everyone on the side of truth listens to me" (John 18:37-38). Whether Pilate really wanted an answer or not, his question rings loudly in the modern mind.

Truth has become an elusive quality, and not only because people are disingenuous and liars. Academics of the last hundred years or so have been obsessed with defining truth in terms of how we use language; truth has become merely the object of wordplay. Whether that is cause or effect of truth's slipperiness doesn't much matter, but the fact that many consider it elusive or slippery does.

The fact is, truth isn't slippery at all. We all know what true means; even the tiniest tots understand the difference between what qualifies as true and what doesn't. What messes up academics, perhaps the rest of us too, is not truth but our lack of trust in our ability to recognize truth when we see or hear it. There are good reasons to maintain a healthy skepticism about our abilities of perception and interpretation: you can believe something is true and be wrong. But truth itself is clear: truth has to do with whatever, in fact, is real.

Since the spiritual, nonmaterial realm is real, it can serve as the basis for truth. Since God and God's kingdom is the ultimate reality, you could respond to Pilate that God and God's kingdom is the ultimate truth.

Definition

A statement, idea, or belief is true when it corresponds to spiritual or material reality.

Quotes

"[Knowledge] involves truth: truth secured by experience, method, and evidence that is generally available." (KCT 18)

"So God uses our self-knowledge or self-awareness, heightened and given a special quality by his presence and direction, to search us out and reveal to us the truth about ourselves and our world. And we are able to use his knowledge of himself—made available to us in Christ and the Scriptures—to understand in some measure his thoughts and intentions toward us and to help us see his workings in our world." (HG 100)

"A thought or statement is true if what it is about is as that thought or statement represents it." (*Veritas Forum lecture, Feb. 13, 2013*)

Other relevant citations

DC 194: God is spirit … "in spirit and in truth.

KCT 18: Belief, by contrast [to knowledge], has no necessary tie to truth … *as if* what is believed were so.

KCT 123: Since there is such a vast nonphysical … as an unquestioned truth …

SD 56: Jesus's sayings … how things are.

VAMPIRE CHRISTIANS

Introduction

Vampire Christians is not the name of an Anne Rice novel, nor a follow-up to the *Twilight* movies. It is a term Dallas used to refer to those who claim to trust Jesus, but who are primarily concerned with getting their sins forgiven rather than with obeying him or becoming like him.

The idea goes like this: Jesus' crucifixion is often understood as the mechanism for God's forgiveness, so if one wants forgiveness one accepts the cosmic importance of Jesus' crucifixion, counting that as the whole of salvation. If discipleship, obedience, sanctification, or transformation are not part or point of salvation, one could be "saved" and go right back to doing whatever one was doing before. Same activities, same feelings, but forgiven. Hence, Jesus' sacrifice—his blood—is something you might partake of without any particular ongoing relationship to him, his work, or his life. As a vampire Christian, you take a little of his blood and go on your way.

Definition

Vampire Christians are those who believe the forgiveness that comes with acknowledging the import of Jesus' crucifixion is all there is to salvation.

Quotes

"A.W. Tozer expressed his 'feeling that a notable heresy has come into being throughout evangelical Christian circles—the widely accepted concept that we humans can choose to accept Christ only because we need him as Savior and that we have the right to postpone our obedience to him as Lord as long as we want to!' He then goes on to state that salvation apart from obedience is unknown in the sacred scriptures. This 'heresy' has created the impression that it is quite reasonable to be a 'vampire Christian. One in effect says to Jesus, 'I'd like a little of your blood, please. But I don't care to be your student or have your character. In fact, won't you just excuse me while I get on with my life, and I'll see you in heaven.'" (GO 13)

"What exactly is a 'faith' that does not naturally express itself in discipleship to Jesus? It would be that of a person who simply would use something Jesus did, but '*has no use*' for him. This is the person I have outrageously called the 'vampire Christian.' 'I'll take a bit of your blood, Jesus—enough to cover my debts—but I'll not be staying close to you until I have to.'" (*Spiritual Formation as a Natural Part of Salvation*)

V-I-M

Introduction

   V-I-M is the acronym for Vision-Intention-Means. It describes the pattern of deliberate activity that is required for any human achievement. Since it is required to achieve anything, V-I-M is—along with grace—the necessary foundation for spiritual formation. When spiritual formation is not advancing, one of these elements—vision, intention, means, grace—is missing.

   Because this pattern is universal for achievement, it must be applied to achieve the interim goals that occur on the way to the big vision, as well as the big vision itself.

   Vision is the mental picture of what life would look like when the goal is achieved. The vision must be thorough and complete enough to sustain inspiration over the long haul.

   Intention is the desire for the vision to be fulfilled, plus the decision to pursue it. While Dallas doesn't explicitly state this, decision may be an ongoing process in itself. That is, until the patterns of activity are settled into your mind and body, you may need to recommit to your decision repeatedly.

   Means are things like the instrumentalities, activities, method, and life arrangements you put into place in order to achieve the vision. It will take research, experimentation and help to discover the means you need, and the means to the end may change over time.

Definition

V-I-M is the general pattern of human goal achievement: vision, intention, means (or method).

Quotes

"If the vision is clear and strong, and the employment of the means thoughtful and persistent, then the outcome will be ensured and, basically, adequate to the vision and intention." (RH 84)

"The vision that underlies spiritual (trans)formation into Christlikeness is, then, the vision of life now and forever in the range of God's effective will— that is, partaking of the divine nature ... What we are aiming for in this vision is to live fully in the kingdom of God and as fully as possible now and here, not just hereafter. This is a vision of life that cannot come to us naturally ... "(RH 86-87)

"An intention is brought to completion only by a decision to fulfill, or carry through with the intention. We commonly find people who say they intend (or intended) to do certain things that they do (or did) not do. To be fair, external circumstances may sometimes have prevented them from carrying out the action. And habits deeply rooted in our bodies and life contexts can, for a while, thwart even a sincere intention. But if something like that is not the case, we know that they never actually decided to do what they say they intended to do, and that they therefore did not really intend to do it. They therefore lack the power and order that intention brings into life processes." (RH 88)

"The vision and the solid intention to obey Christ will naturally lead to seeking out and applying the means to that end. Here the means in question are the means for spiritual transformation, for the replacing of the inner character of the 'lost' with the inner character of Jesus: his vision, understanding, feelings, decisions, and character ... Pure will, with gritted teeth, cannot be enough to enable us to do this. By what means, then, can we become the kind of person who would do this as Jesus himself would do it? If we have the vision and we intend (have decided) to do it, we can certainly find and implement the means, for God will help us to do so." (RH 89)

Exercise—Playing Beethoven

Elsewhere in this *Dictionary* we've utilized the example of playing the piano, specifically Beethoven's Fifth Symphony, as an example of a goal you might want to achieve. Applying the V-I-M structure to that particular goal might look something like this:

Vision: I can play the Fifth with little effort, gaining complete enjoyment from both the experience of playing and the gloriousness of the music itself.

Intention: I will do what it takes to learn to play Beethoven's Fifth.

Means: I will set aside an hour for practice each day, pray for God's assistance, engage a teacher for a lesson a week, listen to a recording of the Fifth once a week, rent a piano ...

The means themselves each have built-in V-I-M structures:

Vision: I arrange my life to set aside an hour for practice each day, maintaining my current important activities, including work and sleep.

Intention: I will arrange my schedule and my calendar to set aside an hour.

Means: I will speak with my boss ... set my alarm clock earlier ...

Here is the exercise. Select one small goal you currently have and write out the V-I-M process with which you will approach it. Remember to make the vision compelling and the means achievable. Also remember that the means may change en route to achieving the vision, so don't fret over getting them just right.

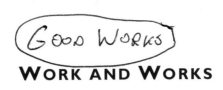

WORK AND WORKS

Introduction

We are making a distinction here that Dallas does not, but because God's work and our co-labors with God are among Dallas' fundamental concerns, it is a distinction worth making.

Notice the use of *work* in the prior sentence. *Work* there refers to an outcome or process of creative effort. For something to be work there must be creativity (that is, generation of something) and effort. Because work requires effort and effort exerts power, work exerts or utilizes power.

Works are tasks and activities taken to effect an end. If you want a clipped tidy lawn, it is almost certain that the work (or task) of mowing will be involved.

Here are both senses in the same sentence: Jesus' works of power were instruments of God's work of salvation.

The point of all this? God has work for each of us, but is generally unconcerned with which specific works we use to do that work. God will empower our efforts—our works—if our work is worthy and we allow God to act. We are to bring God's love and power into every effort we make, and to our work in general.

Definition

Work is an end purpose and the creativity, power, and effort put into achieving it.

Works are tasks, activities, and enumerable efforts.

Work is necessary for salvation; specific works are not.

In the Quotes below, when "work" is used in the first sense, the word appears normally. When the second sense of "work" is intended, it is written in italics.

Quotes

"All *work* should be done as Jesus himself would do it. Our devotion to God is doing the job in sweat, intelligence, love, and the power of God." (DC 286)

"God's speaking in union with the human voice and human language is the primary *objective* way in which God addresses us … This is best suited to the purposes of God precisely because it most fully engages the faculties of free, intelligent beings who are socially interacting with agape love in the work of God as his colaborers and friends." (HG 96)

"[In the discipline of solitude] we must not try to get God to "do something" to fill up our time. That will only throw us back into *work* … " (GO 36)

"The second phase of Jesus' work, in which his disciples were therefore to be apprenticed, was the manifestation of God's rule from the heavens. This was done by words and deeds whose powers lay beyond, or even set aside, the usual course of life and nature … Such *works* were, of course, primarily acts of love done to help those in need. But they were also signs (semeion) or 'indications,' of God's reigning … Though done by human beings, they simultaneously were 'good *works* from the Father' (John 10: 32)." (DC 288-89)

"After we receive the new life, the Spirit continues to move upon and within us to enable us to do the kinds of *works* Jesus did … . The importance of the work of the Holy Spirit cannot be overemphasized." (DC 348)

BIBLIOGRAPHY

Note: All page references refer to the editions and publishers listed below. Other editions will have different pagination.

Books by Dallas Willard

The Divine Conspiracy: Rediscovering Our Hidden Life in God. New York: HarperCollins, 1997.

The Great Omission: Reclaiming Jesus's Essential Teachings on Discipleship. Oxford: Monarch Books, 2006.

Hearing God: Developing a Conversational Relationship with God. Downers Grove, IL: InterVarsity Press, 2012. (Orig. pub. 1984 as In Search of Guidance. Ventura, CA: Regal Books.)

Knowing Christ Today: Why We Can Trust Spiritual Knowledge. New York: HarperCollins, 2009.

Renovation of the Heart. Colorado Springs: NavPress, 2002.

The Spirit of the Disciplines. New York: HarperSanFrancisco, 1991.

Articles and Papers by Dallas Willard

A Crucial Error in Epistemology. *Mind* 76, no. 304 (1967): 513-523.

Apologetics in the Manner of Jesus. *Facts of Faith*. Reasons to Believe, edited by Hugh Ross. Colorado Springs: NavPress, 1999.

Beyond Pornography: Spiritual Formation Studied in a Particular Case. Presented to Talbot School of Theology. September 2008. Available at dwillard.org.

Faith, Hope and Love as Indispensible Foundations of Moral Realization. Unpublished manuscript; available at dwillard.org.

Finding the Noema. In *The Phenomenology of the Noema*, eds. John J. Drummond and Lester Embree, 29. Norwell, MA: Kluwer Academic Publishers. 1992.

Getting Love Right. Presented to the American Association of Christian Counselors, Nashville, TN. September 15, 2007.

The Gospel of the Kingdom. Interview with Keith Giles, August 2005; available at dwillard.org.

Gray Matter and the Soul. *Christianity Today.* Vol. 46, No. 12 (November 18 2002): 74

Intentionality and the Substance of the Self. Presentation manuscript for the Society of Christian Philosophers meeting, American Philosophical Association, San Francisco. April 4, 2007. Available at dwillard.org.

Kingdom Living. Interview with Andy Peck. *Christianity + Renewal*, 2002. Available at dwillard.org.

Knowing How to Acknowledge God. *Westmont College Magazine*, Summer 1998.

Knowledge. In *The Cambridge Companion to Husserl*, eds. Barry Smith and David Woodruff Smith, 138. New York: Cambridge University Press, 1995.

Living a Transformed Life Adequate to Our Calling. Presentation manuscript for the Augustine Group. 2005. Available at dwillard.org.

Marriage and Divorce. With Richard Foster. *Quaker Life Magazine*, 1973.

Moral Rights, Moral Responsibility and the Contemporary Failure of Moral Knowledge. Presented to the Human Rights Conference, IPFW Institute for Human Rights, Purdue University. December 2004. Available at dwillard.org.

On the Texture and Substance of the Human Soul. Presentation notes for Biola Philosophy Group. 1994. Available at dwillard.org

The Professions and the Public Interest in American Life. Lecture notes
for Phil. 141g, University of Southern California, 2007. Available at
dwillard.org

Rethinking Evangelism. *Cutting Edge*, Winter 2001.

Spiritual Formation and the Warfare Between the Flesh and the Spirit.
Journal of Spiritual Formation and Soul Care 1, No. 1 (Spring 2008):
79-87.

Spiritual Formation as a Natural Part of Salvation. In *Life in the Spirit:
Spiritual Formation in Theological Perspective*, eds. Jeffrey P.
Greenman and George Kalantzis, 45. Downers Grove, IL:
InterVarsity Press, 2010.

Spiritual Formation: What It Is and How It Is Done. Unpublished.
Available at dwillard.org

Spirituality for Smarties. Presentation manuscript for Spirituality and
the Academy Conference, University of Southern California,
February 10, 2007.

Subversive Interview - Part 1. Relevant Magazine, June 8, 2004. Available
at relevantmagazine.com.

Truth: Can we do without it. *Christian Ethics Today* April 1999, 12.

Why It Matters If You Are Moral. Presentation at the University of
Southern California to a student meeting, 2005. Available at
dwillard.org.

Books and Articles by Others

Aristotle. Nicomachean Ethics.

Ayers, M.R., "The Ideas of Power and Substance in Locke's Philosophy",
The Philosophical Quarterly 25, no. 98 (Jan. 1975), 1-27.

Bonhoeffer, Dietrich. Life Together: A Discussion of Christian
Fellowship. New York: Harper & Row, 1954.

Calvin, John. Institutes of Christian Religion.

Chesterton, G.K. What's Wrong with the World. London: Cassell & Company, Ltd., 1910.

Foster, Richard. Celebration of Discipline: The Path to Spiritual Growth. New York: HarperCollins, 1998.

Hermann, Wilhelm. Communion of the Christian with God. New York: G.P. Putnam's Sons, 1906. Available at openlibrary.org.

Johnson, Jan. When the Soul Listens: Finding Rest and Direction in Contemplative Prayer. Colorado Springs: NavPress, 1999.

Luther, Martin. Preface to the Letter of St. Paul to the Romans.

Moon, Gary W. "Getting the Elephant Out of the Sanctuary," *Conversations Journal* 8.1, Spring/Summer 2010, 12-19.

Plato. The Republic.

Robinson, Howard. "Substance." In *The Stanford Encyclopedia of Philosophy (Winter 2009 Edition)*, ed. Edward N. Zalta. Available at http://plato.stanford.edu.

8593901R00164

Made in the USA
San Bernardino, CA
14 February 2014